Gillian Bickley

Moving House
and other Poems from Hong Kong
with an essay on new Hong Kong English language poetry

Proverse Hong Kong

MOVING HOUSE AND OTHER POEMS FROM HONG KONG was prompted by happenings and thoughts at a time of change. The poems connect new with earlier events, sights, ideas and information, and draw on both urban and rural environments.

These poems arose within a variety of cultures, in Hong Kong, the United Kingdom, and in several other countries.

Readers from many backgrounds and various ways of life should find points of contact with this poetry, which presents varied experience in words that many will find deceptively simple.

The essay on new Hong Kong English language poetry is the text of a talk given in the English Department Staff Seminar series at Hong Kong Baptist University. This followed the writer's participation in the Third Hong Kong International Literary Festival of 2004, as one of "Five New Scorchers". The essay continues the discussion of writing in Hong Kong, found in Gillian Bickley's first poetry collection, *For the Record and other Poems of Hong Kong*.

GILLIAN BICKLEY, born and educated in the United Kingdom, has lived mostly in Hong Kong since 1970. Her poetry collections include *For the Record and other Poems of Hong Kong* (2003, 2016), *Moving House* (2005), *Sightings* (2007), *China Suite* (2009) and *Perceptions* (2012).

Two collections – *Moving House* and *For the Record* – have been published in Chinese; individual poems have been translated into several languages, including Arabic, Chinese, Czech and Turkish and anthologised in Hong Kong, the Philippines, Romania and the United Kingdom. In July 2014, at the 18th International Festival, "Curtea de Argeş Poetry Nights", held in Romania, she was awarded the "Grand Prix Orient-Occident Des Arts" by the Festival Board. In 2016, In 2016, a selection from her published poems was published in Romania in a bilingual English/Romanian edition, "Poems / Poeme", by Editura Academiei Internaţionale Orient-Occident. Bickley is one of the Hong Kong poets discussed in Agnes S. L. Lam's study, *Becoming poets: The Asian English Experience*.

Her other writings include *The Golden Needle: The Biography of Frederick Stewart (1836-1889)* (1997) and *The Stewarts of Bourtreebush* (2003). She is the editor of *Hong Kong Invaded! A '97 Nightmare (2001)*, *The Development of Education in Hong Kong, 1841-1897* (2002), *A Magistrate's Court in Nineteenth Century Hong Kong: Court in Time* (2005, 2009), and *The Complete Court Cases of Magistrate Frederick Stewart* (2008). With Richard Collingwood-Selby, she co-edited *In Time of War* (2013) (the selected writings, photographs and drawings of Henry Collingwood-Selby).

A long-term adjudicator at the Hong Kong Schools' Speech Festival, she was one of the Adjudicators for the Royal Commonwealth Society Hong Kong Poetry Writing Competition, and one of four voices in the full audio recording of Verner Bickley's three volume anthology, *Poems to Enjoy*; also one of two voices in the five-volume third edition. Her poems are popular with students and teachers for competitions, festivals and grade examinations.

Dr Bickley taught in the Department of English at the Hong Kong Baptist University, as Senior Lecturer / Associate Professor, for twenty-two years. She has also taught at the University of Lagos, Nigeria, the University of Auckland, New Zealand, and the University of Hong Kong.

*Moving House and Other Poems from Hong Kong*   2

# Moving House

## and other Poems from Hong Kong

### with an essay
### on new Hong Kong English language poetry

Gillian Bickley

**Proverse Hong Kong**

Moving House and other Poems from Hong Kong:
with an essay on new Hong Kong English language poetry
by Gillian Bickley
2nd pbk edition published in Hong Kong
by Proverse Hong Kong, July 2016
ISBN: 978-988-8228-53-9
Copyright © Gillian Bickley, July 2016
Available from https://createspace.com/6360601

*Moving House and other Poems from Hong Kong: with an essay on new Hong Kong English language poetry* by Gillian Bickley was first published in Hong Kong by Proverse Hong Kong, 2005 with an accompanying audio CD w. the poet's reading of all poems.
ISBN-13: 978-962-85570-5-9; ISBN-10: 962-85570-5-X

The first edition is distributed (Hong Kong and worldwide) by The Chinese University Press, The Chinese University of Hong Kong, Shatin, New Territories, Hong Kong SAR.
Web site: <www.chineseupress.com>
Also (except Hong Kong) by Aberdeen and North East Scotland Family History Society. Enquiries and orders to The Family History Research Centre, 158-164 King Street, Aberdeen, AB24 5BD, Scotland, United Kingdom. Tel: INT+[0]+1224-646323.
Fax: INT+[0]+1224-639096. E-mail: publications@anesfhs.org.uk
Web site: <http://www.anesfhs.org.uk>

Distribution enquiries to: Proverse Hong Kong, P.O. Box 259, Tung Chung Post Office, Hong Kong SAR. Web: proversepublishing.com

# Preface

## Kinetic Flow
## on Gillian Bickley's *Moving House*

## Chung Ling

It is my fortune to get to know Gillian, for my first year serving at Hong Kong Baptist University happens to be the last year of her tenure in the English Department here. It is also my privilege to be her friend, for she is a graceful, genteel person and a fine poet.

The language of her poetry is lucid, yet there is a kinetic flow beneath the surface. We can sense this flow in reading her poem "What I Wanted to Say" which is about the persona's thoughts on the way to her father's death-bed:

… But, how could I tell you kind things,
without making you know what I
knew? Without making explicit
the implicit cause of my being there
with you, at all?

Now, I have one more thing to remember.

You gave me no space
to say any of this at all,
protecting me still,
as far and as long as
you could; before
yourself
going away,
for good.

A sense of tacit humor flickers often in her lines. In 'Body Language', human conceit is lightly mocked:

We think our cats love us;
and so take pleasure in their arching bodies,
sensuously curving
round our legs.
. . .
and comparison proves,
this book says,
that we are
*furniture*
— *just furniture* —
to cats.

Gillian is also an experienced story-teller, for she is versed in presenting different perspectives. In quite a few of her poems often appears a shift of perspective, so the meaning deepens. In 'Blind Trust' the first stanza is clearly an elegy for her late student who died in a bus crash while the angle in the second stanza is shifted to contemplation on our ignorant complacency when we are in fact bedded in many dangers.

Is this the place, where
our late student's bus
went out of control?—
broke through the barrier and
smashed down through the green
trees… ?

Fatalists, we sleep in the bus,
or lie back in a half-awake daze,
hardly conscious of the risks
our driver takes now,

or those the road-designers took
some years ago.

In this collection Gillian has captured so many glimpses
and moments of Hong Kong. After all, these are the crucial
parts of the moving house, her moving yet stable home —
Hong Kong.

## Commentary by Emeritus Professor I. F. Clarke and M. Clarke

Gillian Bickley writes as she responds to everyday events,
always with the echo of "time's winged chariot" in her
ears. The fact of moving house sends her speeding back
through the moves of a lifetime and forward to the last
move, to the small room of the grave.

The opening poem suggests the elusive presence of the
author, and the deeper themes glimpsed through her
deceptively simple poems.

The variety of human life and the individual response
to life, these are Gillian Bickley's central interests.

The power that invigorates the poems in *Moving
House* is the control of language. In this bare, tight poetry,
no idle words are allowed. Its vocabulary draws on the
base language of essences and epiphanies. The chosen
spare language is the perfect partner for this poetry of
mature experience.

## Author's Acknowledgements

Verner Bickley, my husband, is responsible, both directly and indirectly, for many of the experiences and some of the ideas reflected in this Collection. I am grateful to him, also, for reading through this work and making useful editorial suggestions.

Professor Chung Ling, herself an accomplished poet and Dean of the Faculty of Arts, Hong Kong Baptist University from 2003, is warmly thanked for writing the Preface. Emeritus Professor I. F. Clarke of the University of Strathclyde, United Kingdom, and Margaret Clarke are also heartily thanked for their coupled comments.

Colleagues in the English Department of Hong Kong Baptist University are thanked for organizing and participating in the Staff Seminar at which the talk, "Five New Scorchers Blaze a Trail", was given.

The well-organised group of Hong Kong poets and supporters, meeting monthly under the name, "OutLoud" are thanked for their warm welcome, interest, encouragement and inspiration.

Kavita Jindal's poems, from *raincheck renewed*, are quoted by kind permission of Kavita Jindal. Timothy Kaiser's poems, from *Food Court*, are quoted by kind permission of Timothy Kaiser.

# Moving House and other Poems from Hong Kong

## Table of Contents

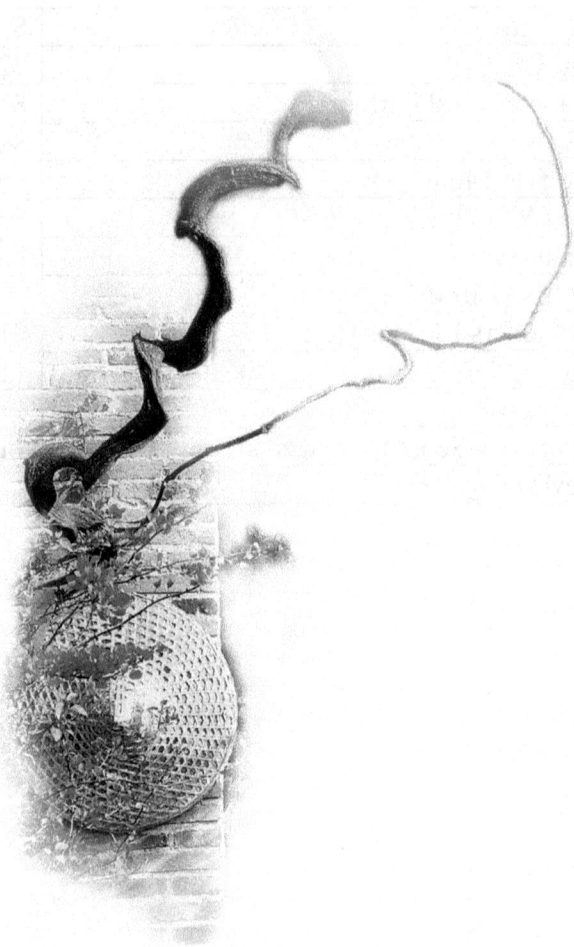

# Snapshots

My poems are snapshots of Hong Kong;
and sometimes ?
as you know ?
a photographer's image
appears in his pictures;
caught by the reflection of glass,
in a mirror, or in someone else's
eyes.

But you can never
be
absolutely
sure
that you've seen him or her,
or even
the subject chosen, or seen.

21 April 2004

# Moving House: Memento Mori

Flats come in many sizes.

Five thousand square feet, I've never had:
two thousand five ?  three thousand five ?
perhaps, I have:
first when employed by Hong Kong U,
and again, some years later,
when married to you.

But you retired in ninety-two.
The flat got smaller.
Now I'm retiring too.

Downsizing again!

One day, the space
we
each
occupy
will be five foot six times two.

March 2004

# Washing: I

When Richard Boyle[1] designed his Chiswick House,
he thought about heights and light,
vistas, avenues and elegant proportions;

but human needs, not at all! ?
No kitchens, no bathrooms, no lavatories.

In castles, built in medieval times,
at least there were those
still-evil-smelling chutes
in the corners of rooms,
where you emptied the contents
of your chamber-pot ...
or someone did it for you.

Today, it's washing that's ignored,
or rather the drying of the washing.

Look around! No pink gins on the balconies,
afternoon teas, or frills;
but ugly rows of undistinguished washing.

Drying clean linen in public!

March 2004

# Washing: II
*(Repeat 'Washing: I' above and add this verse.)*

We don't all have a dear little fishing boat,
newly varnished with bright paint;
spunkilly breezing through Hong Kong harbour,
gay shirts flapping in the breeze!

March 2004

## Experimental Method

If you're capable of "What-if" thinking,
steer clear of craftsmen
who work in the home.

They will never agree
to do what you want,
until after they've done
what they want,
and found it wrong.

30 April 2004

# Walking New Paths

Walking paths
we find exciting,
thinking of those
who've walked there
before. Where were they going?
What were they thinking?
Did they see this flower,
admire that view, rest and
drink from the cool stream,
just here?

But a new path,
prepared by
developers,
or rural authorities,
is almost not worth treading,
simply going from A to B,
with no companionship
from previous travelers
? not even a mountain goat ?
accompanying us on our way.

10 April 2004

# Body Language[2]

We think our cats love us;
and so take pleasure in their arching bodies,
sensuously curving
round our legs.

But I have read a book,
which explains
the body language of cats.

They make this movement,
when recognising other cats.
They do that,
responding to furniture;
reacting to chairs and tables and stools.

And comparison proves,
this book says,
that we are
furniture
? just furniture ?
to cats.

\*

In the DB bus to Tung Chung,
tall pilots stand, their short sleeves
implying their strength, and
imperviousness
to changing climes.

They were on the bus first, 'though still
obliged to stand; and they
move for no-one,
keeping the comfortable fit, they've found
between the luggage rack and their friend's seat;

resting on nearby passengers, when the bus
rolls them round, as if
they think them
merely furniture too.

March 2004

# Metal Birds

Driving to and from Tung Chung,
down the new road,
at the airport end . . .

Metal eagles poise to land in rows
in a variety of postures
among the new bushes of hibiscus
and the carefully trimmed weeds.
Others ready themselves for take-off.

*What's the idea?*

Is it a way of saying,
"Even bigger birds are near?
"Metal" (what type of metal?) "Boeing seven four sevens,
"seven three sevens, airbuses, are also
"landing—taking off in careful rows—
"somewhere quite near"?

Or, something quite different,
is it a way of warning eagles off?
"Do not fly here!" . . . "Too many eagles already!"

and so,
stopping them
from flying into engines,
interfering with radar,
and preventing
*us*
from making
a safe landing?

March 2004

# Ma Wan *or* Contrasting Views on Access

Why call "Ma Wan", "Park Island"?
"Ma Wan", if you go by road,
"Park Island", if you travel by boat?

On one side, facing south south west,
in a pretty half-circle, facing the sea,
casually grouped with low-rise buildings,
in a variety of colours,
the *old* Customs Station;
manned by Manchu China
in the late Ching Dynasty;
quite similar still to how someone
captured it, in an old photo.

And on the other side,
paradoxically facing east,
a *modern* complex: high-rise buildings,
with club-house, marina,
shopping-centre, and ferry pier.
—"Quite nice really,
and not too far from Hong Kong Island",
as an estate agent might say.

*Old* Ma Wan
charged a fee to *boats* passing through.

Park Island, with closed road and bridge,
forbids *cars*.
"Access for permit holders only",
the signs proclaim.

It has its own little navigation light,
plenty of rocks; yellow floaters,
surfacing the water;
nets beneath.

I wonder, do the rule-makers
check for holes each day?

Or do they wait
to keep out *danger*
for the first *il*literate shark
to kill the first *sub*literate
early-morning
swimmer of the year?

2004

# Transport Contrasts[3]

Bleached wooden props protrude,
like dead trees,
from the salt inlet,
next to the site
for the new subway station,
at Yam O.

Between a few ? but only a few ?
tree trunks lie,
piled up. A few
ash-coloured fishing nets and low dusty buildings
also suggest that boats may still be made here,
from time to time.

     *

Think of those proud, bold
two-eyed junks, loftily
sailing through the wide seas,
manned by a small crew,
and all the unexpectedness
each day could bring them.

And think about those blind, hurtling caterpillars,
stuffed with commuters, almost unmanned,
scurrying their unsurprised
and unsurprising way,
underground.

March 2004

# Self-absorbed[4]

Have you noticed
how the person in front of you,
boarding the MTR,
with an empty seat in their sights,
dawdles as they secure it,
blocking your way,
preventing
you
from gaining any, still empty seat,
that could have been yours?

2004

# Private Time

The journey to work is still
private time in some aspects at least.

Some of us somnambulant.
Some eating their breakfast.
Some completing their toilet.

A big city gent is picking his nose.
An airhostess paints her long red nails
(surely suggesting
scant intention
to put up our cases
—hang a fur coat, maybe).
Small boys revise their homework.
Little girls flirt with their neighbours.

When do we put off this privacy
and put on our public selves?

When we enter the
"Paid Area" of our lives
(not our transport connections)
perhaps? ?

21 May 2004

# Transported

Any number of unknown
young men
have rested their head
on my shoulder,
on public transport, as they
helplessly
embrace their sleep.

Have
you
ever
resisted transports,
on transport,
too?

2004

# Fear

A scaly silver lizard
flicks at my foot,
and my fear leaps,
before I see
the tethered bubble-wrap,
caught in the pavement guard.

What must the people of Iraq,
the British and American soldiers
be feeling now,
confronted by towering
danger,
they
suddenly
grasp
for real.

2004

# Mormon Temple, Cornwall Street, Kowloon Tong: I

Balancing right foot forward, the left heel
raised—partly tip toe, then—
wearing a simple, waisted tunic,
with loose folds at the neck,

he raises his golden trumpet

not, as one might expect, high,
facing the sky;
but outwards,
calling across
the dwellings and shops, places of work and play,

trumpeting
the good news.

We need not hear it,
only see the simple act,
speaking sweet volumes to the observant eye.

March 2004

## Mormon Temple, Cornwall Street, Kowloon Tong: II[5]

Neo-classic, ziggurat-like box,
your neutral lines and careful
curves shutting in secrets;
in-turned on your truths
with some blind windows too,
you arouse curiosity,
but slightly repel . . .

until the eye travels up,
sees the gilt ball, the narrow pyramidal column,
balancing there; and, at its peak,
another, smaller, gilt globe,
supporting the human herald,
that justifies it all.

March 2004

# Blind Trust[6]

Is this the place, where
our late student's bus
went out of control,
broke through the barrier and
smashed down through the green
trees on the steep hill;
crashing into the villagers' homes,
leaving them still traumatized?

Fatalists, we sleep in the bus,
or lie back in a half-awake daze,
hardly conscious of the risks
our driver takes now,
or those the road-designers took
some years ago.

March 2004

# Road Safety: I

I don't think the black and white markings
will save us.
Nor the short piece of wire fencing,
seeming an afterthought
on the road-defining wall.

These will not save us passengers.
These will not save the dog trotting by,
the men repairing the road,
the retired gent taking his daily jog.

All that will save us is you,
bus driver, you and your skill.

Do you get enough rest?
Can you go home when you're ill?

Are you calm and comfortable,
not too challenged or bored;
happy in your work,
interested in all of us on board?

Please don't kill me!
Let me get home to my husband
once more!

March 2004

# Road Safety: II

"Look left!" the road sign says.

But I'd look right too.

You never know when some
lost soul,
crazy driver,
or skate-boarding child
will bear down,
thoughtlessly,

on you.

3 April 2004

# Original Sin

Written after reading the news of the death of the Thai
epileptic, listed in the *Guinness Book of Records* for
spending the longest consecutive time penned up with
snakes.[7]

What was it really that killed you,
Boonreung Buachan?
The snake that bit you?
Or those who thought
the convulsions the cobra caused
"only" a fit?

Did it go further back?
Would no one employ you,
four hundred miles north of Bangkok,
because of your frequent fits?

Could you read?
Was it you who learnt of Guinness
and longed for fame?
Or did some Thai Papa Mozart,
in your family or town,
see their chance?
Forced you to earn
their place in the world
for them?
We can only guess.

Snakes have a sinister record;
but so do some people too.

22 March 2004

# The Monster of Lonmay[8]

Written after reading a newspaper report, stating that the
family roots of the American pop rock singer, Elvis Presley
("the King") are in Lonmay, Scotland.

Elvis Presley hails from Scotland?
I can well believe the tale,
although the Scottish sceptics
don't count on any sale.

"It won't be very big", they say,
"not like the Loch Ness Monster".

But, looking down the years,
this is what I clearly see: . . .

Cairness House restored, quite grand,
coffee,
crumpets,
afternoon tea,
and a charming pipe band,
for the likes of you and me;

hordes of tourists
paying money
to admire
Playfair's Palladian interior,
not designed
for inferiors,
at Lonmay;

its ice house nice again,
waitresses busy
farmers in a tizzy,
because of
the Monster of
Lonmay.

Rock, rock, rock!

Lonmay Rock!

What a shock!
Better take stock
and set up shop,
farmers of Lonmay!

Pop goes the Presley!

Forget sheep!

Better breed
Elvis look-alikes,

quickly!

March 2004

## Modern Fates, here confused with the Furies of Ancient Greece[9]

Hairdresser,
Kind one,
your scissors cut hair,
not our lives,
just yet.

Dentist,
Kind one,
your drill bores teeth,
not our lives,
just yet.

Doctor,
Kind one,
your scalpel slices skin,
not our lives,
just yet.

The doctor will certify
when we die.

The dentist will confirm our grim grin.

The hairdresser will comb our hair,
one last time.

But our nails will keep on growing! . . .

March 2004

# Past Present[10]

We miss the past because we came from there:
people and scenes and places, and ways of
doing things:

old women, mumping[11] their lips in the sun;
old men, eating their breakfast,
outside the Museum of Heritage,
at Shatin;
university students,
cherishing school friends,
from primary and secondary days.

And I, do I miss the past, too?

Not yet, not yet.

I embrace the present,
in embracing you.

But I
surely know
the past is where we also come from;
and where we're going, too.

March 2004

# Christmas Letters from Afar[12]

What was it that Virgil said?

"Like falling autumn leaves . . ."?

The ghosts of dead souls
pressed close around Æneas,
their visitor,
drawing life from his sacrifice of blood,
as he visited
the dark depths of the past;
seeking one soul,
asking it to speak to him.

And here they come, fluttering through the mailbox: ?
souls from our pasts, briefly warmed by unselfish thoughts
of us (and others),
stirring us also with new insights,
as we remember them,
think of them,
briefly visit
their present lives,
through our contemplation
of them and theirs;

remembering our lives,
when they were with us
always.

Noted 2003; completed 2004

# Street Cries

When I lived in Conduit Road,
occasional street cries
delighted, disturbed:
"Buy my fresh mangoes,
"lychees, apples-o!"
Buy into my world!

Thirty years ago, a man's voice cried,
"Knives! Bring out your blunt knives!
"Knife-sharpener-o! Hurry outside!"
Buy into my world!

Yesterday, I walked again
down Conduit Road.
Strangely, a man's voice still cried there.
But what goods, what service does he sell? ?
He pulls a trolley bearing only ropes.

"New ropes!  Hangman here!  I will hang
"you if you want!"

Buy out of your world!  Buy out of your hopes!

24 March 2004

# Fortune Teller

Many years ago,
I visited the Temple at Tai Wai;
crossing a small bridge over an open drain;
and viewing, but not turning,
the windmill that gives good luck.

The old wooden temple is still there,
but inaccessible;
hidden behind a new temple, built some yards away:
a taller, grand stone edifice,
with high surrounding walls
and daily flocks of tourists, following flags.

Outside are rows of fortune-tellers' booths.

At one sits a woman,
fairly young, shrewd and sensible,
but also business-like.

Student ambassadors
volunteer to interpret,
as your beautiful granddaughter
seeks advice, on family and studies.

"Ten dollars a question",
the fortune-teller says.
The girl's three questions become two.

"You're very sure of yourself,"
the pronouncement comes.
"Think of things sometimes from others' points of view;
"but spare some money for yourself sometimes."

A clever woman!  The hint
that thirty dollars is not too much
to pay for her advice. The flattery.

But also, the good advice.
Counsel which,
from others, was ignored;
from her, was wondered at,
accepted,
taken aboard.

Not a bad place to take
your adolescent sons and daughters,
when they
won't listen to you!

March 2004

# Marriage

Written after meeting poet Jane Bhandari (English, married
to an Indian), who had lost her beloved husband
unexpectedly some years previously.

Marriage is for life,
ideally,
they say:

but,  also true,
marriage is for death:

death of selfishness, independence, and carelessness;
death of loneliness, and single nights.

And, after death, there are
all the long years, which we
may devote
to considering
and carrying out
the living wishes
of our other.

This part, Miss Brooke  (Dorothea) avoided.
Fiction gave her a cop-out.

But Jane Bhandari is not
part of a George Eliot novel, and
she cannot.[13]

2 April 2004

# Mutuality

You shed an eyelash. It irritates my eye.
You have a headache? I have one too!
Your eyes need testing? Mine are dim!
Your prostate needs some soothing? I must get up now!
Your dentist summons you? I should go there too!

I learnt from my Mother
to expect a husband to know certain things
for both: people's names, historical events;
but you have learnt from me this ignorance,
forgetting what you knew.
Now neither of us knows
all that we should and could and did.

I lived on bread and cheese,
"good" lunches at canteens.
You enjoyed rich sauces and curries,
but advocated greens.
So now (theoretically)
we eat fish, rice, oats and beans,
reminding each other periodically
that chocolate is bad for us.

Twin trees, closely planted,
reach up to the light; reach out to each other.
One extends, the other yields.
One sheds leaves, the other roots
deeper. The wind blows. They embrace.
Each other's anchor in the storm.

Completed 26 May 2004

**Easter Egg** *or* **"Please clean up your afterbirth after you!"**
*or* **Crossed Twigs (Crossed Messages)**

"Help cleaning our planet!"
the plastic wrapper says,
displaying a hapless Easter chick
in a pile of scratchy twigs.

What's the chick supposed to do?

Make a besom of the twigs
and set to work,
the moment it's out of the egg?
Sweep up
the broken shell of its afterbirth?

And are we
supposed
to do something similar,
too?

3 April 2004

# Muzak

I don't know about you.
But, for me,
some muzak is
the saddest sound
in the world.

In fast food stores,
does it
aim
to chase us out,
so more people
can be seated?

If so, it certainly fails.

We sit, saddened, sobered, and soul-destroyed;

unable

to summon

the will

to leave.

3 April 2004

# Her Good News *or* Good News for Modern Woman

She jerked and reached her hand
towards her stomach,
patting it.

Was that a baby kicking there?

But no. She pulled out her throbbing . . .
mobile phone;
and answered it.

April 2004

# Scene in the Street: Handing Gloves

Buying from a hawker,
I carelessly dropped my gloves and walked away.

Out of the blue, a French woman
tapped my shoulder,
following me
up the escalator,
to join the Deli France queue.

"Two," she said.
"Usually it's one",
handing them over,
delphically,
but also delicately.

And that was all she said.

Noted c2002; completed 2004

## Scene from a Bus I: Bird's Eye View

In silhouette, above us,
birds sit in a long row,
stretched out along a concrete overpass.

2004


## Scene from a Bus II: Sweeping Changes

The street sweeper
uses her mobile phone
standing next to her piled-high trolley.

2004

## Freudian Tea Cosy

You know those fluffy, full-bodied cats,
with striped tails, arching
over their backs,
as they turn and look at you, from
children's books, cushions,
tea cosies and table-mats?

As I lay in bed, but before I slept,
one came to life before (or behind)
my closed eyes;
and then . . . its striped tail became
a striped snake,
about to detach itself
and strike.

6 & 7 April 2004

# Nail Clippers

You know those small nail clippers?
They only clip a part of any nail,
leaving a small part attached,
most inconveniently;
sometimes embedded behind the nail that's left?

You have, too?

But have you ever had such a sliver of sharp nail
suddenly release itself
and shoot right in your ear?

You have, too?

Entrepreneurs out there, here's an idea!
"Ear protectors to wear, while clipping nails!"

March 2004

## Sleeping Head

On nights when light
still traverses thin curtains,
look beside you!

Do your eyes alight
on a sleeping head
on the pillow beside you...

the sheet neatly pulled up and smooth
and no body
in view?

Does it seem absurd, to you, too?

6 & 7 April 2004

# Knowledge and Purpose

When you play a violin,
you place your fingers
on the strings, here and here,
"making your own notes".

When you steer a dragon-boat,
you stand in the stern,
holding an oar in the water,
making it your rudder.

When you measure a length,
you stretch your fingers out to a span,
you walk heel to toe, heel to toe,
making yourself (if not man) the measure of all things.

But you must know what your length is,
what your destination is,
what music you want to make.

11 April 2004  (Easter Sunday)

## Easter Stunt Man

You break out of the egg,
from your three days'
suspension
between life and death;
when the yoke of your mystery
adequately fed on the protein
of your confidence.

And now you knock at our hearts,[14]
wearing a crown of thorns,
holding a lantern, for always;
wishing that your earthly father,
the carpenter,
would come to fit the door handle
that would let you in.

11 April 2004 (Easter Sunday)

# Humility

What was it he had found?  A dynosaur's
print in the hills? Signs of the earliest man?

Something like this.

Something stupendous and marvelous,
out of an ordinary man's way.

But what I remember is him; his total humility.

"What did you feel like,
"when you found it?"
the television reporter asked.

And the Italian, or Frenchman, said, "A bit afraid.
" A discovery, too big for me.

"And then I thought,
"maybe it is God's gift."

Noted 2003; completed 2004

# Progressive Movement[15]

The old man leant into the breeze,
jogging in very slow motion
the other side of the railway track,
and the man-made hill the other side of him.

And it reminded me, so many
years ago, a pillion passenger on a
Kawasaki bike, in New Zealand,
crossing a wide, sunny, windy plain,
leading to a place called "Bull",
I burst out laughing, when,
as it seemed to me,
the power of the bike
and the opposing
force of the pretty strong wind
were so justly balanced,
that I felt we would be perpetually there,
seeking to cross the golden, hot plain,
but constantly held back,
suspended for ever,
between two equal powers.

And I thought also of Alice,
and the Red Queen's precept, that,
in some circumstances, it takes
a great deal of running,
even to stay in one place.

13 April 2004

# Stumps

The stumps of slender branches
protrude from the water.

Where are the roots, from
which these amputations
have been sawn or sliced?

Have you seen the forest with lopped off bodies?

Its low stumps remind us of limbless
human bodies, also
sacrificed to others' desires.

13 April 2004

# Conferees

They tumble down the steps
stout puppies, eager for their food.

Were they as eager as this, for the
mental sustenance
their conference
promised them?

Or did the glossy brochure,
the call for papers,
the abstracts of so many words,
and the emailed proposal
lead them only to this?

A chance to chat, to shine,
make new friends, forget close foes;
a free three-course hurried lunch,
and a little variety
in the daily
grind?

March 2004

# Solitude[16]

One thirty- or forty-plus man,
standing;

palms together, raised over his head, slightly forward;
praying.

A steep stepped slope close behind.
A wide, man-made canyon and a steep slope before.
Hot sun. No shade.

Was this where the accident was?

Not an empty gesture;
but projecting concentration.

Small against the man-piled slope;
small, compared with the expanse
of concrete high-rise dwellings,
in front and below.

But what significance he
gives the other human figures!

 A small fragmenting group,
construction workers going home.
None of them briefly reaches it at all.

One lone man,
his feelings, thoughts and prayers,
against a vast sea of dead concrete
and other material concerns.

2004

# Filial Daughter at Tung Chung

Across a metal table,
bearing a single cup of coffee,
she sat, her jeans' leg bottoms
unfashionably frayed,
opposite her wheel-chaired mother.

Mother and daughter gazed at each other,
seeing and not seeing such familiar folk;
and when one spoke,
the other hardly thought an answer
was in order.

The daughter's eyes took in
the young girls,
with their smooth made-up faces,
talking excitedly
about their own concerns and lives.
But she also saw another middle-aged woman,
sitting there, alone.

What did she wish or speculate?

Or was she simply deciding,
it was time to take  her mother home?

6 & 7 April 2004

# Moving Emotions

Smartly dressed
in well-cut  black trousers and light jacket,
carrying a not very full, also black shopping bag,
the thirty-something woman
slowly crossed the road,

dragging one foot
and shuffling it to meet the other,

dragging one foot
and shuffling it to meet the other.

She seemed unanxious,
accepting of this,
her very personal mode of motion.

Perhaps a lesson to us all,
who cannot wait ten seconds,
without a strongly negative emotion.

6 & 7 April 2004

# E. F. B.

The old man perched on the railing,
waiting for a bus;
holding in his hand a large fabric bag
with the lettering squarely facing us.

"Environmentally Friendly Bag"
with the letters "E", "F", "B"
emphasized in bold.

Is there any other significance he sees?

"Elderly Friendly Bus", perhaps?

I'm afraid he'll have to wait a very long time.

6 & 7 April 2004

## Music and Message

Young man with the good voice,
modestly reintegrating with the Christian choir,
singing Easter music,

after your confident solo;

holding your head back, mike high,
letting your voice
show the meaning of the words,

Maria Callas would have
liked you;

rebuking one  home-town singer,
in the massed choir accompanying her,
with the words,
"I have some friends in the audience too, who
"expect to hear Me."[17]

8 April 2004

## Chinese Cowboy with Lilies

He stood at the Tung Chung bus-stop,
with a bunch of heady, white, pollen-laden lilies;
the cut of his jeans, shirt and hat, echoing
Texas, U. S. of A.

But his face showed him a home-town boy,
back on an Easter visit.

How did he achieve this confident mixing of cultures?
Was it all unconscious absorption?

If so, I hope no-one  ever makes him
recognize his differences,
shocking him out of his  easy placidity,
and making him capable of  writing a few lines like this.

21 April 2004

# Mao Hair Cut

It's not a good idea to cut your own hair;
even when you've stitches in your skull
from some excision,
following long sojourns in foreign parts;

even less so, in countries,
where Chairman Mao's image is well known.

For then, the over-short side,
away from the parting,
will be taken as modeled on Mao's familiar hair-style;

and that short cut of yours irreversibly perpetuated.

April 2004

# Em-[Brace]-let

Sturdy little boy at the bus-stop,
wearing thick, clean, pure cotton shirt and shorts,
what woe impels you to scream and cry
and cling to your grannie's thigh
so much and so long?

Is she taking you somewhere you don't want to go?
Are you leaving someone you don't want to leave?

And your grannie, what does she feel,
her thigh embraced by this screaming boy
so much and so long?

Ignoring him doesn't help;
nor shouting at him;
nor pointing a stern finger;
nor swinging him roughly off his feet;
nor sitting him on a rail
and threatening to drop him in a ditch;
nor pretending to take off his shoes.

Will the bus never come, to break their impasse?

Do they still remain at the bus stop, locked
in their deeply felt (expressed or repressed) emotions:
the seemingly obdurate rock of his safety
and the tumultuous waters of the child,
whose bracelet clearly shows
that, any time he almost drowns,
someone, however apparently absent-mindedly,
will lift him out.[18]

23 April 2004

*Moving House and Other Poems from Hong Kong 66*

# Language Lessons

An old man with heightened colour
approaches near me,
gesticulating, laughing, talking,
even when I say, "m sik teng", "I don't understand".

He points down the waiting area, where
a tall, big boned, round faced, mildly wrinkled
and slightly limping old woman
comes into view,
and arrives slightly out of breath,
laughing too.

So now I know
what her husband was telling me.
"My wife's gone to the wrong place again.
"I told her she was wrong. But she never
"believes what I say."

So they sit next to me,
and we wait together,
they chatting to me companionably;
and me repeating it again,
holding and patting her hand:
"m sik teng", "m sik gong",
"I don't know how to speak [Cantonese]".

When I emerge from my appointment,
they chat to me again. The old man
wants to see my next appointment slip,
nods wisely and returns it.
 (I guess that's what he does
when his wife emerges, too.)

And the old woman wants to know,
if the two lengths of ankle support in my hand
were given to me inside.
"Keuih da bei ngoh", I say,
"She gave it me", and the old couple nod,
quite satisfied.

Honestly, you don't need language at all,
just experience of your fellow man,
context-driven communication,
and willingness to believe you can
"understand and speak".

But I tell you this. If one needs motivation
to learn a really difficult foreign language,
an endearing old couple in a public hospital
certainly make the considerable effort
seem entirely worthwhile.

1 May 2004

# Osteoporosis Clinic

So we sit here, mainly the working or
lower middle class, interspersed with
some a little bit different,
clothes more elegantly casual, or with gold glasses,
trimmed with tortoise-shell, on the nose.

We wait for five minutes with the doctor,
who will stop our bones from breaking,
keep our backs straight, and help us walk
without hobbling, or grimacing.

What it is to be old,
with the time to wait,
with the space to take measures to put right or avoid
what our hasty youth made wrong, or impaired.

Mainly women; some men
(none with ties, even those
whose shirts are white and sleek),
we sit meek and resigned;

showing a bit of life,
only when negotiating a place in the queue.

2004

# Change with Constancy

*Goddess of the Sea, Tin Hau, speaks.*

I have been here for a long long time
facing out to sea, protecting the villagers at Chek Lap Kok.

When the foreigners first came in their big sailing ships,
I was already here.

When the cannon sounded in the Tiger's Mouth,[19]
and the mandarins' power was challenged by the West,
I observed the outcome and the consequence ? more ships
that sailed the sea.

And now my villagers are moving me away ?
the men that fish my sea,
the women that mourn their men folk's loss ?
taking me with them to Tung Chung on Lantau,
where they also go.

I am wearing my silk robe, bordered with pearls, and
my head-dress also is bedecked with pearls.

Before boarding the boat, we take a last look
round the village, saying farewell. The people are
sad to leave. But the big machines that fly
need another place to land; and they want this place of ours.

As for us, the sea (not the sky) is our element. We can find
another place to merge with it, facing its bounties and
banes.

The villagers have changed; but not so much, that they
forget the ways their ancestors have followed.

*Moving House and Other Poems from Hong Kong   70*

The clothes they wear are sometimes foreign clothes;
but they eat the dishes that they always ate,
*baak choi*, *choi sum*, rice, fish and other vegetables.

The children learn both western knowledge
and our Chinese ways.

But their hearts are mine.

Begun 199[4?]; completed 2004

# Sacrifices

What a surprise to find a beheaded owl
in Kowloon Tong, outside the Beverley Hotel!

In Ibadan, in Nigeria, I once saw
the head of a dog, placed judiciously upright,
centred in the middle of the road:

 a sacrifice to Ogun, deflecting that
god of the road
from taking this dog-killing driver's life,
for his first sacrifice of the day.

But this owl, Symbol of Pallas Athene,
goddess of maidens? Was some
sad beau symbolically seizing
the maiden-head of that evening's blind date,
hoping to make symbol true?

Noted c2002; completed 2004

# A Pure Devotion

It was still there,
the new shrine, that I first saw yesterday.

The gods had nibbled the biscuits in the
thoughtfully opened packet;

but had left the apples, wrapped sweets and
oranges,
for another day.

How ones heart is moved!

Pleased at the thought, that
here is offered thanks for happiness given,

sad in case of a mute plea
for a need to be met,

warmed by the possibility
of an absolutely pure devotion.

December 2003

# Professional Pride or Tunnel Vision

Have you noticed
how hairdressers
focus their attention
on the back of the head;
proudly showing this
in the mirror, for you
to admire their completed work?

As for me,
I'm more concerned
as to how my face looks
from the front and the sides.
Does the style show my better features
and soften the worse?

And what about cleaners,
intent on getting a shine;
ignoring the scratches they make
in that expensive picture window? Or
the workman, who uses a parquet or marble floor
as his surface for work?

Then there's cricketer Lara, scoring
three centuries and eighty runs,
a world record, and his team,
seven centuries fifty;
but the match was only a draw.[20]

Lear turned his attention to fashion.
The expensive clothes his daughters wore
barely kept them warm.[21]

Women in particular wear shoes
which, ultimately, ruin their feet.

And we all know the saying,
"Operation successful; the patient died".

30 April 2004

# What I Wanted to Say

After I got the phone call, booked the
flight and was safely seated,
with the seat-belt dutifully round me,
fastened at all times,

I thought about you and what I
should say when I saw you ?
already confined on what was certainly
your death-bed.

"The right to know."
This was one of several rights
the web-site listed,
under "hospice" and "pain".
"The right to talk about it" was another.

I remember how I coughed, night after night, one year,
with whooping cough,
and every year afterwards;
and that you were patient and kind.

I remember that you took me out,
one Sunday afternoon, to learn
to ride my new bike. And when I fell off,
said, "Don't tell your Mother!"

I remember that you gave me money
to pay for music lessons,
against my Mother's very clearly-expressed wish.
I remember once, myself an adult,
already away from home some twenty years,
you waited up, for me to come home,
after a mild evening out.

I remember you lent me your car for two weeks,
another year, when I was again home on leave.

I remember and value your praise for two books I wrote.

These were some of the things I wanted to say.

But, how could I tell you kind things,
without making you know what I
knew? Without making explicit
the implicit cause of my being there
with you, at all?

Now, I have one more thing to remember.

You gave me no space to say any of this at all,
protecting me still, as far and as long as
you could; before yourself going away,
for good.

Noted 2001; completed 2004

# Self Image

"It doesn't look nice", you said,
gazing in the mirror at the wrinkled skin,
hanging in folds from your thin buttocks and thighs;
thinking, I am sure, of the shapely legs that my father
admired
and which, as a girl, you kicked overhead,
practicing routines you'd seen in, "No, No, Nanette".[22]

And indeed it doesn't seem kind
that comeliness can drop away
with appetite; leaving so little encouragement
to survive; self-image being
all that widows may have left,
when facility and abilities decline so much;

leaving only sad spirit and sharp
intelligence; perceiving what
is gained instead and irremediably.

10 April 2004

# Human Flowers

Flowers can last a long time
if you change the water,
cut the stems sufficiently and often,
downsizing containers,
as the stalks diminish in size.

Some people shrink too, needing
smaller clothes as they age.

Our bodies spontaneously reduce,
harbouring the essential juices we've got left.

8 April 2004

## Almond Petals

Driving down the road
away from you . . .

Almond petals weep.

But the white plum trees still
raise slight arms to the sky,
never doubting their late flowers
will bear fruit.

Saturday, 29 March 2003

# Self-assertion

Newly transferred from hospital,
what did you mean,
when you walked
naked at night,
down the corridor
in the Nursing Home?

And how did you do it?

Were you clutching on to the hand-rail,
that ran everywhere along the wall?

Were you saying, "Here I am,
"still a woman, not a parcel,
"with my own ideas and feelings.

"Deny me if you dare!"

Noted 2003; completed 2004

# The Photograph

You stretch out your hand to us,
sitting in the wheel chair,
wearing your wide-brimmed straw hat,
with the broad ribbon, elegant
in the two-piece summer dress,
you wore for your ruby wedding.

Unable to converse,
either with spoken or in written words,
struck newly with this unexpected
affliction and frustration,

your look is full of communication.

But what is it you say, pleasantly
reaching out towards us, just so?

"Here I am!  Hello!  I'm still here!
And I'm greeting you before I go!"?

And where do you send your message?

Simply across the grassy space,
between you and your photographer?

Or out through the grassed turf,
between the ashes you are now
and the flesh we still are yet,

Gazing at this photograph and all you meant.

2 April 2004

# Visiting the Funeral Parlour

Small and still,
you lay there;
your thoughts removed
to another plane;

beyond me,
beyond us all,

hieratic. . . .

Our concerns
not your concerns
any more. . . .

Our lives
of no interest
to you
any more.

The immensity
of your absence
and your presence

is a lesson
in respect.

31 March 2004

# Where Now?

If you opened your eyes
and saw where you were,
Would you have said,
"Where am I now?"
angry, or puzzled, or wondering,
taking a strange thing on board?

Would you have wanted a mirror
to see what you looked like?
Wanted colour
to temper your pale smooth skin?
Wanted a heater
to take away
the bitter cold?

Would you approve the pink brocade gown?
Notice your wedding ring gone?

Would you have thought of the stages to come?
The light dark box and the hammered nails?
The jolting movement  to the car
and the slow ride
through streets you could not see?
the grocer's,
the butcher's, the post office;
your neighbours' houses;
your house;

then voices
your daughter and her husband beside?

And then the church, slow pealing of bells,
the service, the hymns, the eulogy.

*Moving House and Other Poems from Hong Kong   84*

Would you wonder
how many
flowers there were in the car and above you?
Tried to gauge how many people were there?
Did they wear black? Were there tears?

Did you fear the end
of your final journey;

the smaller party

and then

the consuming

fires?

17 May 2004

## Loss *or* Never More[23]

No-one again will

ever

be so interested
in what we do;

will read our letters
with such intensity
of interpretation;

will ring instantly
when hearing we are ill, or in hospital.

No-one will stand at the gate
waving and waving
as we pass out of sight
leaving the country.[24]

No-one and never


ever more.

31 March 2004

# Kindness

*(a fragment)*

That night I dreamt
I was penniless

and my Mother came,
stretching out her hand to me,
offering a full bag
of sovereigns, or half sovereigns.

And I woke up,
sobbing at such kindness,
from beyond the grave.

31 March 2004

# Generation Gap

How sad it is
that you sacrificed time and money
to give me
what I did not want.

How sad but glad.

How sad it is
that what I gained
and wished to share with you,
you would not take.

How sad but glad.

Did you think?

Noted 2003; completed 2004

## "Keep it for Memory"

"Keep it for Memory"
my grandma said,
handing me a portrait of herself:
a youngish woman,
whom I had never seen.

A gold locket hangs
on an amply-laced blouse,
which she probably made with her own
skilled fingers.

The soft hair is piled up,
around and on top of her head;
and the dreamy eyes
linger on her future.
Her engagement portrait.

And my grandfather faces her now
in his separate silver frame,
across the dressing-table.

His ample, softly wide moustache
decorates a handsome face
above a neat collar and a well-cut suit.

A good-looking pair,
whom I remember
quite differently.
Ah! The holiness of the heart's affections!

17 May 2004

# Five New Scorchers Blaze a Trail[25]

A Talk given at a Hong Kong Baptist University Department of English Language and Literature Staff Seminar on Monday 3 May 2004[26]

On 8 March this year, the Third Hong Kong International Literary Festival kicked off with a performance by five Hong Kong English language poets, chosen because each had brought out a new book of poetry since the last Festival in 2003. The support and response from the English Language media, the public, and bookshops was strong. *The South China Morning Post* (SCMP) published a lead story,[27] with front page banner, the day the performance was scheduled. As for the performance, as the *Sunday Post* reported, "The Fringe Theatre was packed . . . when the festival kicked off with five local poets".[28] The SCMP review, "Performance poetry steps into the literary limelight", was supportive, introducing comments from members of the audience. "Performance poetry, as the many first-timers who watched Five New Scorchers at the Fringe Theatre . . . found out, is about ordinary people giving you a glimpse of their world. . . . 'It's great to experience it . . .. It was a rare privilege to hear a poet read a piece in the way they had envisioned when they wrote it.'" [29]

Following the performance and review, Matthew Steele, of Dymocks bookshop chain, wrote to each of the poets, "Congratulations for bringing local poetry to the attention of the masses."[30] He followed up, by arranging and promoting another reading, "Scorchers Reignited", held at Dymocks, International Finance Centre, on a Saturday afternoon (24 March 2004). The advance publicity for this further event again referred to the fact that the Festival Performance had been sold out.[31]

Professor John Carey ("former chief judge of the Man Booker Prize and a revered critic with *The Sunday Times* of London for twenty-five years"[32]) attended the Scorchers performance, and found the readings an excellent introduction to Hong Kong (private conversation with the present writer; and others also reported that Professor Carey said the same to them). Carey's response is not surprising, since the collections as a whole refer to the professional and private lives of the poets (including secondary school and university teaching, and participation in Hong Kong Society), and they include observations of people seen and related to in public places, as well as reactions to Hong Kong's urban and rural landscapes. Some poems face more towards an expatriate life and concerns, and some address episodes in cross-cultural relationships, including cross-cultural marriages and family relationships. So, overall, a representative balance is achieved by the group, taken as a whole, not only as seen from non-Chinese eyes, but reporting, or seeking to view, Chinese lives from the inside.

At the time these books were published, all five poets had been Hong Kong residents, from a minimum of a couple of years to thirty years or more. Two poets are Indian, one having lived also in London, England. Two are British — one born in Libya — and both have experience of living in a handful of countries. One was born in the USA but grew up and attended University in Canada.

In order of publication, the books are: *echolocation* by Mani Rao, *For the Record and other Poems of Hong Kong* by Gillian Bickley, *raincheck renewed* by Kavita Jindal, *Food Court* by Timothy Kaiser, and *Clearing Ground* by Martin Alexander. Is there any sense in which, taken together, these books form at least a part of the choir making up a Hong Kong voice? Does the success of these books indicate a change in the Hong Kong English

Language literary scene? Does it contribute towards the image of internationalization that Hong Kong currently seeks to present?

## Introduction

By making my leading question one that refers to "a Hong Kong voice", I of course raise the question of definition. What *is* "a Hong Kong voice", both as applied to an *individual* writer and to a *group* presence? — The answer to this question can, of course — partly depending on the participants — involve a discussion of several different factors, including place of birth, place of residence, ethnicity, language used, languages known, social and family contacts and activities, duration of any period of residence in Hong Kong, commitment to Hong Kong, subject matter, style, attitude, tone, literary tradition followed, even political allegiance. It also requires a prior discussion (not to be entered into here) of, "what is Hong Kong"?

The first question — "What is a Hong Kong voice?" — is similar to one of those I grappled with in the early 1970's when compiling a bibliography of Hong Kong Creative writing in English.[33]

Overall, looking back at what I wrote twenty-six years ago, I seem to have included in this bibliography writings in three main categories: firstly, writings by Hong Kong residents, whatever their subjects. Secondly and thirdly — in the case of people who had previously lived for at least a period of time in Hong Kong — I included such writings as are either *about* Hong Kong or which *refer* to Hong Kong, and also other writing by this group, when it seemed plausible that it owed some part at least of its subject matter or inspiration to Hong Kong.[34] Addressing my different task today and the question, "What is a Hong Kong voice",

*Moving House and Other Poems from Hong Kong 93*

I would consider all three of these categories as making up part of the "Hong Kong voice".

It could be suggested that a similar view is implied by Dino Mahoney, in his introduction to an anthology of poetry, compiled from readings at OutLoud, the monthly Hong Kong poetry reading organized by the group of the same name. Quoting and borrowing one-time participating poet, Alden Bevington's, phrase, he suggests that a Hong Kong voice is that of any writer whose windows, "open or once opened on to the streets of Hong Kong".[35] I would amplify this statement a little, to clarify that the rural, as well as the urban, scene is also included: "a Hong Kong voice is that of any writer whose windows 'open or once opened on to the streets [or landscape] of Hong Kong'".

I would also expand the definition more substantively: "a Hong Kong voice is, also, any writer who, consciously or unconsciously, takes Hong Kong as his or her subject, or finds in it, inspiration."[36] However, I think I would need to consider, on a case by case basis, whether to include any such writings, from a time when the writers had never set foot in Hong Kong. (The reason why I would consider such writers at all, is because it is perfectly possible to write about a place, or to be inspired by a place, never having been there. Indeed, as mentioned later, the image of Hong Kong as conveyed by the various writers, now under discussion, who really were residents at the time these various collections were published, is, of course, their individual view of Hong Kong — their individual construct — and one could argue, philosophically, that it is not Hong Kong at all.) I would also include those, like one among the group under discussion, Martin Alexander, who, Clare Tyrrell reports, "wouldn't call himself a Hong Kong poet".[37]

Broadly speaking, inclusiveness rather than exclusiveness seems to provide a more valuable basis for defining a Hong Kong voice, or components of the Hong Kong voice, if the objective is to express and project Hong Kong to the global community, or indeed, to those members of the Hong Kong community itself who have an international as well as local and national perspectives.

My answer to the first question, then — Is there any sense in which, taken together, these five new collections of poetry form at least a part of the choir making up a Hong Kong voice? — is clearly, "Yes". And the main part of my talk will be simply to give an indication of each book's content. I hope you will take the time, later — if you have not done so already — to read these books, to decide for yourselves what the nature and thrust of their contribution is, to the complete orchestra that is Hong Kong's voice, mostly of course expressed in the Chinese language.

The five collections are, in fact, very different from each other and each writer has a very distinct voice. But, as Dino Mahoney writes, of the OutLoud anthology published in 2002, "a disparate blend of voices is the true song of the city".[38] And indeed, as Hong Kong becomes more international, this statement will obviously become increasingly more true; and any continued growth in the writing and publication of literature with a Hong Kong voice, in the international language, English, will be a means of supporting this growth of an international ethos.

Initially, I will discuss these five collections, in alphabetical order of writer's family name.

Martin Alexander's *Clearing Ground* is arranged in three untitled sections. Among the seventy-eight or so poems, there is a mixture of personal and universal topics with reflections and reactions to external events and landscapes. Although only one includes the word "Hong Kong" in the title ("Still Life in Hong Kong" (p. 92)), a few have titles, which those who know Hong Kong would recognize as also referring to Hong Kong ("Hoi Ha" (p. 31), "Big Wave Bay" (p. 43), "Taipa temple"(p. 64)), and several others explicitly refer to Hong Kong places, locations or institutions. (These include: Lower Cheung Sha Beach, Lantau (p. 30), Wanchai Road (p. 46), Cloudview Road (p. 48), Stanley (p. 68); Ninepins, Sai Kung, Loi Lam's restaurant (p. 98); Hong Kong advertising (p. 44), Fat Angelo's (p. 51), Island School (p. 70), and the Mass Transit Railway (p. 78).) Intimates may recognize other poems also as referring to Hong Kong people or circumstances. Alexander's subjects do, however, also relate or refer to the other locations where he has lived, spends time, or has traveled, including Mainland China, Spain and Vietnam.

Gillian Bickley's *For the Record and other Poems of Hong Kong* presents its sixty poems in chronological order, with no sectioning. Nevertheless, the poems have two main groups of subjects: one, people, birds, trees, the natural and man-made worlds seen and experienced in Hong Kong; and the other, personal events which were what they were because the writer lives in Hong Kong. The first group includes observations and reflections on Chinese and westerners as they or the writer/persona criss-cross Hong Kong on foot or by public transport. There are accounts of stage performances, including manifestations of both Chinese and western culture. In one poem, the voice is that of a Chinese ancestor, watching his living family come to visit him at Ching Ming Festival (pp. 56-59). The title poem, "For the Record" (p. 12), written almost three decades before the return of Hong Kong to the government of Mainland China, reflects on old photographs of Hong Kong (where the shutter speed was too slow to capture any but posed or posing human subjects), and wonders whether non-Chinese Hong Kong residents will be given any place in future Chinese consciousness or history. A poem written very shortly after 30 June 1997, when Hong Kong was returned to the administration of Mainland China ("Swallows", pp. 60-61), ends with an epiphany, reflecting the imagined emotions of all those of any nationality who left Hong Kong prior to the change, feeling that they were leaving their real selves behind.

The thirty-four poems in <u>Kavita Jindal's *raincheck renewed*</u> are separated into five sections.

"Living in the Well" describes personal states of mind and feeling — sometimes reflective, sometimes violent — often expressing a conflict between desire and ambition on the one hand and restraint and control on the other. This section concludes with, "Optimism" (p. 16): "I never yet fell/ In so deep and dry a well / That there was no water to be found/ When I scratched beneath the arid ground." The only indication of what may be an explicit glance at Hong Kong is in the poem, "And Wrap It Up, Again" (p. 15), where we find: "The voice of my memory / noodle-like[39] / unravels on the polished floor / and nips at my ankles."

"Aspiring to be a Tai Tai" presents a series of experiences encountered in the Hong Kong worlds of designer-label shopping and the leisured women who buy these labels. The tone is satirical and clear-sighted, and the self-observant attitude is at different times assertive and self-effacing.

"The Ones that Bite" are poems focusing on separate incidents and moods in what appear to be several emotional and sexual relationships (not necessarily the writer's own). The poems are modern and international in perception and expression.

As the title suggests, the cluster, "My Father's Life in Mine", is about the writer's (or persona's) relationship with her father. In the poems, she seeks to understand her father's life and character, relates incidents in their relationship, and muses on the extent of her likeness and unlikeness to him, giving voice to some of her own personal objectives and desires.

"Conversation Pieces" contains poems on varied subjects, not explicitly related to Hong Kong, and quite likely deriving from other locations. Some reflect on the writer (or persona) herself, as well as on other individuals. Some of these poems react to and reflect on major events, which came to international awareness, close to the time when these collections were published. In "Orange, burnt" (p. 47), the writer imagines being present at the October 2002 bombing in Bali. "That's War" (p. 49) reflects on politics and war, and the individuals who create and suffer from them. In its twenty-three lines, "Shards" (p. 50) ambitiously tackles the varied topics of mutual misunderstanding, dealing in funerary antiques, and Hong Kong's new Disney theme park.

Timothy Kaiser's *Food Court*, true both to his North American birth and upbringing, on the one hand, and his decade of Hong Kong residence and his Hong Kong family, on the other hand, is divided into two sections, "East" (about 65 poems) and "West" (about 45 poems). In the first section ("East") the name, "Hong Kong" appears in one amusingly provocative title, "The Night Gong Li[40] Came to Hong Kong and Governor Patten[41] Slept on the Couch" (p. 36) and other titles contain Hong Kong references that are obvious to those who know Hong Kong adequately: "Still Life: Wan Chai At Night" (p. 25), "Show and Tell on a Slow Mong Kok Night" (p. 31), "On the Banks of the Shing Mun River" (p. 63), "Demolition Next Door to the Chung Chi College Library" (p. 77), "Happy Valley Dreams" (p. 85). The poems themselves include descriptions of Chinese Festivals in Hong Kong ("Mid-

Autumn Festival" (p. 59), "Dragon Boat Races — Sha Tin" (p. 60)).

References to Hong Kong history — interestingly (and having regard to the writer's Canadian upbringing) suitably presented from a Canadian perspective — are signalled by some titles, "The Battle of Wong Nei Chong Gap — December 1941" (p. 73), "old man to his caged bird — July 1$^{st}$, 1997" (p. 55), "Lowering Jack" (p. 57) and "Handover Ceremony — July 1$^{st}$, 1997" (p. 58), but such references are also to be found in poems with no such signal (e.g "equanimity", with its reference to imperial armies and revolutions (p. 28)).

The people Kaiser writes about include people observed as he moves around Hong Kong, but they also include his Chinese wife and Hakka in-laws, who are presented in personal and domestic contexts. As well as giving his own reflections, Kaiser imagines what they might think and feel, and what their past circumstances might have been (see e.g. "Minibus 14M" (pp. 26-27)). There are also poems, which describe personal incidents in a Hong Kong setting (e.g. "As The Pendulum" (p. 86) and "Chorus" (p. 87)).

Beyond these, Kaiser also reaches for understanding of human behaviour in general (e.g. "Morning Mariner" (p. 79), which sees the morning newspaper as having a kinship with Coleridge's Ancient Mariner — "If I have learned anything/ . . . / it is not to ask why the albatross/for if not the albatross/there is always something beautiful/something innocent/to kill").[42]

The poems in the section, "West", are very obviously from the same sensibility as the later poems in "East", and clearly suggest why the poet was open to a cross-cultural marriage and life. "West" contains many narratives and reflections on family and personal life and on education, against an occasionally glimpsed background of international events, including the Vietnam War. Kaiser links his experience both with that of others he knows or has seen and with what he has read in books ("on snow" (p. 101)). He empathises with the different experience of others and compares his trivial concerns of a young adult with the concurrent hard lives, for example, of political exiles ("on and off" (p. 104)) and economic immigrants ("Prairie Percussion: Wong's café" (pp. 108-109)).

Mani Rao's sixth collection, *echolocation*, consists of thirty or so untitled poems. Although intensely aware of the external world, they refer to no obvious location, other than the poet's own inner life and intellection, prompted by external stimuli (including other persons) and the universe from which she takes her soundings; and, as an indication of the scale of her referrents, the only named person is the Director General of the United Nations, Kofi Annan (p. 28). She creates her own world and offers us momentary entry through her poems.

The five new collections taken as a whole
In spite of their distinct voices, there are interesting networks of some similarities between and among the writing in these five new collections. A few of these, but only a very few, will be indicated, very briefly, here.

In these collections (and my comments are restricted to these), four (Alexander, Bickley, Jindal and Kaiser) write about named close family members. Two (Bickley and Kaiser) show awareness of and interest in Hong Kong history and the changes in the Hong Kong environment. Three reflect on their places of work (Bickley on University students and campuses; Alexander and Kaiser on secondary school students). Or, we may say that four of the five do this. For Jindal reflects on the worlds of Hong Kong socialites and company wives, which — since she herself is a company wife — may be considered her own "places of work".

Four (Alexander, Bickley, Jindal, Kaiser) reflect on Hong Kong people they know and do not know. (Interestingly, a greater number of these poems are about people not known, but seen in the street or other public places, or on public transport. While this reflects the reality of Hong Kong's multi-sectioned society, with little daily equal social contact between all strata within the different ethnic groups (in what part of the world does this happen?), it nevertheless shows the poets' desire to come at least into imaginative contact with those they may never know.)

Varying threads of cultural difference are described or indicated (e.g. Kaiser, "birthday bird", where a rare injured bird is disposed of by his mother-in-law because, "not good have / Caged bird on birthday" (p. 67) and "To Cool the Fire" (p. 82) which describes the making of newborn puppies into Chinese medicine as "the horror"). Cultural difference is wrestled with (e.g. Bickley, "Differences" (pp. 64-66), and Kaiser, "Dragon Boat Races — Sha Tin" (p. 60)) and sometimes transcended.

Some of these poems present understanding, empathy, fellow feeling or deep concern, as well as sympathy at humble losses and tragedies (Alexander, "The colour of mourning" (p. 35); Bickley, "Janus" (p. 31), "Ching Ming Festival" (pp. 56-59), "Swallows" (pp. 60-61); Kaiser, "anniversary present" (p. 32), "eradication" (pp. 38-39) and "The Chinese Side of the River" (p. 68)).

Some collections have poems on similar topics. Bickley and Kaiser (both with years spent in non-urban environments) each have poems about caged birds. (Bickley, "Comparing Notes" (pp. 26-28); Kaiser (e.g. "Coal Mines of the City" (p. 76).) In the work of each, the moon and the landscape feature.

Alexander, Bickley and Kaiser each have poems about preparing or writing poems. (Alexander has several such poems (e.g. "Hunting for poems" (p. 14), "Writing" (p. 29), "How not to write a sonnet" (p. 41). Bickley has two ("Welcome" (p. 11) and "The Reason for it" (p. 50).) Kaiser's, "Demolition Next Door to the Chung Chi College Library" (p. 77) shows him preparing to write poetry by observing others; for often these observations, as we see in the collection, later become poems.)

Elaine Ho describes some of Tim Kaiser's poems as, "actualizations of dialogue between the poet and people he knows, and doesn't know". (Elaine Ho, p. 12.) The same is also true of some of Bickley's poems, although she addresses natural objects and creatures as well as people.

Form
Most of the writing is in free verse. However, in one example of pattern or concrete poetry ("unnatural selection" (p. 90)), Kaiser partly echoes devotional English poet, George Herbert's use of the shape of wings on the printed page. Of the five poets, Martin Alexander shows the most interest in subjecting himself to the discipline of stricter forms, such as the sonnet and haiku (pp. 54-57). Consistent with this, perhaps, is the fact, already mentioned, that quite a few of his poems are on the act of writing poetry itself. Bickley's final poem, "Flower de Lune" (p. 105) and one of Kaiser's (untitled, p. 62) have a similar spareness of form.

Voice
Most, but not all of this work seems to be written, either in the poet's own voice or in that of a persona which derives from some aspect of the poet's own ideas and personality. — It is always dangerous, of course, to derive biographical facts from a writer's work! — A notably successful

example among the exceptions is Alexander's, "The ageing biker's boast" (p. 17). The Hong Kong Arts Development Council's reviewer has praised Bickley's "Ching Ming Festival", where the voice is that of a Chinese ancestor.

Editing
Kaiser's useful glossary explains both Hong Kong and North American terms (pp. 149-150). However, occasionally, there are North American references, which any later edition might wish also to explain (e.g. in, "cheering on the Ethno Centrics" (p. 143)). Bickley introduces some poems by giving their occasion and adds notes on any intertextuality.

Additional material
Mani Rao's collection is presented, embellished merely by its unusual book design and the list of her previous published collections.

Martin Alexander includes an author's "Preface". This, with the "Dedication" and "About the Author" adds background about the author himself and the process of publishing his collection, *Clearing Ground*. Kavita Jindal's dedication and acknowledgements, together with the brief notes about the author, do the same for her collection, *raincheck renewed*.

The collections by Martin Alexander and Timothy Kaiser each include a critical essay by a different member of the English Department at the University of Hong Kong (namely, the Head of the Department of the time and a previous Head of the Department).

Additional to the paragraphs on the cover flaps about the author and about the book, Gillian Bickley's *For the Record* includes the text of a talk given by the writer to the English Society of the University of Hong Kong in 2002. "Literary Odyssey in Hong Kong: a Personal Narrative" interweaves a sketch of Bickley's own writing career with commentary on her own knowledge of the Hong Kong English language literary scene from 1970 up to date. It opens with a "Preface" by the President of the Hong Kong Schools Music and Speech Association (HKSM&SA), which takes the opportunity to make the point, particularly to that Association's constituency, that, "literature is what we all may produce".[43] Referring to the fact that the publisher was offering one copy of the book to secondary school members of the HKSM&SA, she writes: "I am confident that it will be a useful means of encouraging teachers and students to consider Hong Kong — their own city and their own countryside, themselves, their own families and fellow citizens, flora and fauna — as valuable subjects for literature. Additionally, I hope that teachers and students will be confirmed in their understanding that acquiring excellent skill in the English Language is a community service as much as it is a personal advantage. We need to communicate with the outside world, and to give them our own many visions of Hong Kong, to win friends and understanding within the international community. How better to do this, for the next many years, than through excellent English?"[44]

Intended Audience
In keeping with this link with Hong Kong schools, *For the Record* reaches out to readers, not necessarily dedicated poetry readers, including non-native speakers. The two CDs, packaged with the book, containing the poet's reading of all sixty poems in the collection, are additional means to seek an extended audience, which has in fact been achieved.

The collections by all five writers are of course self-expression and in that sense are addressed to the poet himself or herself; but all also imply a readership of similar personalities and sensibilities, with similar education and cultural knowledge and broadly similar moral training and outlook.

**Does the success of these books indicate a change in the Hong Kong English Language literary scene?**

The answer to this can be rather brief. Yes! To my own knowledge, there has never been any long-term territory-wide English language literary scene in Hong Kong. And this is supported by Louise Ho, writing in about 2002, who says, "There is no English-language literary community [in Hong Kong]".[45] Indeed, in spite of recent experience, one of the five "Scorchers", Mani Rao, as reported by Clare Tyrrell, in the SCMP, feels more or less as Ho: "I don't think there's an English-language literary scene in Hong Kong yet . . . although there's more noise and more books and events than four years back. It's a small circle."[46] But today and for the past few years, as it seems to me, largely sustained by the energy and ability of a few individuals, an English language literary scene is struggling into existence.

This assertion can be supported by reference to the response of the media, the audience at the Literary Festival, and the response of the manager of a bookshop chain, as briefly sketched earlier in this presentation. All show a sense of something new, a welcome departure from the past.

Whether this change can be sustained and translated into the burgeoning of a solid and secure literary scene will depend very largely on the ability and willingness of the same few individuals (or of any replacements, which the normal fluid movements in and out of Hong Kong society may bring about) to maintain the momentum. It will also depend on the avoidance of fragmentation brought about by any of a variety of factors. It will depend on the support of bookshops, funding agencies, schools, universities, examination bodies, speech festivals, and the general public. To a significant extent, to reach its maximum widest public, it also depends on the assistance of English-Chinese translators. Even those who can read English include many who need the reassurance of a Chinese translation before accepting that they can read and understand at least some modern English language poetry. And I would like, here, to acknowledge the generosity of Dr Simon Chau, who has translated all sixty poems of *For the Record* into Chinese.

## Does the success of these books contribute towards the image of internationalization that Hong Kong currently seeks to present?

Again, my own answer is rather brief, "Yes". The fact that five non-Chinese residents have published collections of poetry in Hong Kong, containing work about Hong Kong, work informed by, inspired and educated by Hong Kong, must create an impression, beyond Hong Kong, of a certain degree of maturity in Hong Kong society.

Additionally, to the extent that the work is accessibly on explicitly Hong Kong subjects, it also serves to extend the image of Hong Kong within the consciousness of international readers.

And this is so, even though, as briefly mentioned earlier, more sophisticated commentators have rightly pointed out that the Hong Kong projected in these works is a construct of the writers. Writing of Kaiser's *Food Court*, Elaine Ho speaks of, "A world of lived cultural experience which is named 'Hong Kong'".[47] And she also writes, "His observations, like the best poetry, create their own world".[48] Of Gillian Bickley's *For the Record*, David McKirdy writes: [Bickley's] "Hong Kong is both a universal and a personal one and like Italo Calvino's book *The City* . . . captures a Hong Kong of the mind; the one city that we all share as a physical space against the myriad cities that we experience and perceive distinctly as our own."[49]

Thirdly, and finally, it seems the case that work which reaches beyond the particulars of Hong Kong culture and Hong Kong geography may also — only initially paradoxically — result in a better appreciation of Hong Kong. Writing about Canadian poetry, Tim Kaiser makes a point, which can be adapted and applied to Hong Kong poetry too. In the poem helpfully entitled, "Bruce, Al, and Gus at the Spiritwood Saskatchewan Male Poetry Appreciation Club Weekly Meeting" (pp. 110-111), he describes a conversation where the fine American writer, Emily Dickinson's writing is dismissed and poetry asserted to be "a man's game" (p. 110). Then the writing of a male Canadian writer is held up as a model of good poetry, but the content leads to an objection:

Alright, now listen up you know-it-alls to this here highlight reel
Of a poem by Early Birney [i.e. Earl Birnie]:

> When I come to the grave-cold maw of the bergoschrund... reeling
> Over the sun-cankered snowbridge, shying the Caves
> In the névé . . . the fear, and the need to make sure it was there
> On the ice . . .

Whoa, Gus, whoooooa.
Just hang on one lousy goddam minute.
That's the whole thing I been telling you guys all along
There are just two things wrong with Canadian poets:

First — Snow
Second — Ice
I mean, just think about it.
Ya think ole Lawrence Ferlinghetti, jersey retired,
MVP captain of the Red, White and Blue
Sittin' in his San Francisco bookshop
Chewin' the butt of a yellow HB
Gives a bergoschrund about Canadian Snow and Canadian
Ice....
© Tim Kaiser, 2004

As pointed out here by Kaiser, while poetry on local subjects, or referring to contents of the local scene, serves to interest the local community in poetry and in creative writing and does also extend and enhance awareness, internationally, of the locality concerned, there is also the danger that poetry which refers to localities which are not those of readers will lead to a loss of interest among more than some.

Perhaps, to garner additional international respect, or respect in different quarters, poetry needs to transcend and cease to refer explicitly to the local, so that it can be read as literature, not simply as the literature of a particular place or even of a particular time.

Indeed, among the poems in these five collections are some that do achieve this: poems, which focus on the age-old and universal human conditions and concerns of family, love, and death and the more modern additional concern as to the nature and contentious rights of the individual personality. There are such poems by Kaiser, a few by Bickley and Jindal, some by Alexander, and most of Mani Rao's are in this category.

There may be a difference of opinion about this. Awarding bodies or local critics and experts may consider that explicitly local poetry is what should be supported, as well perhaps as poetry where the influence of local residence can at least be argued. Shirley Lim evidently felt this when, in her review of Peter Stambler's Coming Ashore Far From Home,[50] she implied disagreement with the Hong Kong Arts Development Council's award in support of the publication of this selection from Stambler's collected works. — This collection, if I have read it correctly, does not mention Hong Kong at all (except in giving the address of the publisher and when referring to Stambler as "Professor of English and Head of the Humanities Program at Hong Kong Baptist University"), but it does dwell imaginatively on European and North American subjects and localities.[51] — In my own early days in Hong Kong, I myself seem to have thought somewhat similarly to Lim. In the Introduction to my bibliography of Hong Kong creative writing in English, already mentioned, I made the following observation, which now seems to me rather strange: "it is very much a feature of Hong Kong that many people do not accept their residence here as real. Consider, for instance, Edmund Blunden's output during the time that he was Professor of English at the University of Hong Kong. Far more of his total output when in Hong Kong was on English — or even on Japanese subjects — than on Hong Kong".[52] And I made this point when discussing what writings to consider as "Hong Kong creative writing in English". Blunden's collection, A Hong Kong House, is of course very well known and Louise Ho speaks of it today as, part of the "canon".[53]

To repeat a point made, earlier on in this presentation, when focusing on a different question, it seems very clear to me today that inclusiveness not exclusiveness is what is required. If one were to draft a programme, or, "blaze a trail", for the development of a local literature, it seems to me that both the explicitly local and the universal should be viewed as eminently desirable. And this is a point broadly supported by Louise Ho in her ex cathedra introduction to City Voices (Hong Kong University Press, 2003), edited by Mike Ingham and Xu Xi, which begins by reporting a literary conference held in Downing College, Cambridge, in 1999, at which Salman Rushdie, "Held forth expansively on cosmopolitanism" and a, "well-respected Welsh poet . . . claimed 'the local' versus 'the global' as his fortified ground".[54] As far as Hong Kong literature is concerned, the "five new scorchers" have added their marks or blazes to those already notched by others and in previous publications, including (in the case of three of the five) in their own earlier published work, and these give indications of possible routes on both local and universal paths.

One final point, it seems to me that writers, or their editors, or their publishers, need always to remember that we need to mediate our work to readers. If we want readers to accept certain work as Hong Kong poetry, then it makes sense to present it as such. For the Record does this very clearly, in the title, "For the Record and other Poems of Hong Kong". The collection of poems itself sustains this description by the fact that many of the poems are on explicitly Hong Kong topics. Tim Kaiser's Food Court, although including poems about Canada, places his Hong Kong poems first and, indirectly therefore, gives the reader the opportunity to see in the Canadian poems the roots of the sensibility which led him to form his Hong Kong identities, thus making them also relevant as expressions of a "Hong Kong voice". The title of Peter Stambler's Coming Ashore Far from Home could strike a chord with all the many Hong Kong residents (Chinese, as well as those of other nationalities), who have come to Hong Kong from a different place, where they have put down their primary roots. But the response of his reviewer, Shirley Lim, indicates that this was not enough.[55] Evidently, more mediation than this was necessary; or more evidence, in the poems themselves, of sensibility at least slightly modified by his Hong Kong sojourn. And later poets, editors and publishers will probably bear this lesson in mind; but at the same time, taking care not to lose in the process the international and universal dimensions of Hong Kong works.

# Bibliography

Poetry Collections Discussed
Martin Alexander, *Clearing Ground*, Hong Kong, Chameleon Press, 2004.
Gillian Bickley, *For the Record and other Poems of Hong Kong*, Hong Kong, Proverse Hong Kong, 2003.
Kavita Jindal, *raincheck renewed*, Hong Kong, Chameleon Press, 2004.
Timothy Kaiser, *Food Court*, Hong Kong, Chameleon Press, 2004.
Mani Rao, *echolocation*, Hong Kong, Chameleon Press, 2003.

Criticism, History, Journalism, Personal Communication
Gillian Bickley [see also Gillian Workman], "Literary Odyssey in Hong Kong: a Personal Narrative", Talk given to the English Society of the University of Hong Kong, 19 April 2002, *For the Record* (*q.v.*), pp. 107-114.
*The Economist*, "For crying out loud", 27 March 2004, pp. 81-82.
Nick Gentle, "Performance poetry steps into the literary limelight", *South China Morning Post*, 9 March 2004, C3.
Elaine Yee Lin Ho, "Foreword", in, Timothy Kaiser, *Food Court*, Hong Kong, Chameleon Press, 2004, pp. 11-14.
Louise Ho, "Foreword", in, Xu Xi and Michael Ingham, eds, *City Voices: Hong Kong Writing in English 1945 to the Present*, Hong Kong, Hong Kong University Press, 2003, pp. xiii-xiv.
Mike Ingham, "Writing on the Margin: Hong Kong English Poetry, Fiction and Creative Non-Fiction", in *City Voices*, *op. cit.*, pp. 1-15.

Douglas Kerr, "Afterword", in, Martin Alexander, *Clearing Ground*, Hong Kong, Chameleon Press, 2004, pp. 105-110.

Shirley Lim, "Coming ashore for a wander" [Review of Peter Stambler, *Coming Ashore Far From Home*, Hong Kong, Asia 2000, 2000], *South China Morning Post*, 4 February 2000.

Dino Mahoney, "The OutLoud Story", *Outloud*, Hong Kong, XtraLoud Press, 2002, pp. 1-8.

David McKirdy, "Personal and Universal" [review of Gillian Bickley, *For the Record and other Poems of Hong Kong*], in, *The Asian Review of Books*, 2003.

Rosie Milne, "under cover", "The Review", *Sunday Post*, 14 March 2004, p. 9.

Matthew Steele, email message to each of the five "Scorchers", 11 March 2004.

Clare Tyrrell, "Stanza and deliver", *South China Morning Post*, 8 March 2004, C5.

Gillian Workman [now Gillian Bickley], "Bibliography of Hong Kong English Language Creative Writing", in, *Asia/Pacific Literatures in English*, edited by Robert E. McDowell and Judith H. McDowell, Washington, DC, Three Continents Press, 1978, pp. 85-115.

Xu Xi, "From and of the City of Hong Kong", in *City Voices, op. cit.*, pp. 17-26.

Websites

Scottish Civic Trust on behalf of Historic Scotland, "Buildings at Risk Register for Scotland", http://www.buildingsatrisk.org.uk

Wikimedia Foundation, Inc., *Wikipedia*, http//www.en.wikipedia.org/wiki/Moroni_(Mormonism)

# Notes on the Poems

[1] Richard Boyle, Third Lord Burlington, designed Chiswick House, which was completed in 1729. He was assisted in the design of its grounds by William Kent and Charles Bridgeman. Burlington was influenced by Inigo Jones, the famous British architect, 1573-1652, who had introduced the "Palladian style" into Britain. Apparently Chiswick House was not intended as a residence, but nevertheless has been called, "a masterpiece of domestic architecture".

[2] DB (Discovery Bay, Lantau Island) is within commuting distance of the Hong Kong International Airport at Chek Lap Kok (opened 1997), and hence home to many extremely pleasant airline and airport personnel.

[3] The completed MTR station (overground here), serving the Disney Resort, is now called, "Sunny Bay".

[4] MTR: Mass Transit Railway (underground railway; subway).

[5] The writer viewed the statue of the angel from an Anglican Protestant Christian perspective. Later she learnt that a statue of the angel, Moroni (in life the son of Mormon after whom the Book of Mormon is named) stands on the top of many temples of the Church of Jesus Christ of Latter-Day Saints (LDS), facing east, and that images of Moroni are commonly used as an unofficial symbol of the LDS.

[6] See also, 'Solitude' in this collection.

[7] Boonreung Buachan, a Thai national, was listed in the Guinness Book of Records in 1998, for spending the longest continuous time penned up with snakes (seven days in a glass box). He died aged thirty-four, after a cobra bit him during his daily snake show. He went into convulsions after he was bitten, but people thought it was an epileptic fit and did not send him to hospital until he was already dead.

This news was broadcast on Reuters Daily email Report, 22 March 2004.

[8] Lonmay is a small village in Aberdeenshire, North East Scotland. Cairness (built 1791-1797) is a grand mansion out in the countryside, which changed hands in about the 1990's and began to be refurbished from then onwards. James Playfair (1755-1794) was the original architect.

[9] The writer has confused the classical Fates (three blind women working with a spinning wheel, one of whom cuts the thread of lif) with the Furies (Erinyes) (whose names were later propitiatingly changed to, "te kind ones" (Eumenides)).

[10] Inspired by the following sentences in an assignment onf Laurie Lee's Cider with Rosie, written by Rita Lee Po Yu, student of Discursive Prose (ENG 1170), 2003/2004, taught by the writer: "We miss the past because we came from there. As we get older, we have more memories and are even more reluctant to change."

[11] A neologism of Elizabethan, Thomas Nashe ("and never mumped crust more"), which appears in his pamphlet, *Piers Penniless, His Supplication to the Devil*.

[12] For Æneas's visit to the Underworld, see the Æneid, Book VI, by Publius Vergilius Maro (Virgil) (70-19 BC).

[13] Dorothea Brooke, the heroine in George Eliot's *Middlemarch*, is asked by her scholar husband to promise to compete what she has come to see as his futile and superceded work The Key to All Mythologies, should he die with the work uncompleted. Dorothea asks for a little time to think it over, goes for a walk in the garden to do so, and after a struggle, decides to agree; but before she rejoins her husband in the house to convey her decision, her husband has died and Dorothea therefore considers she has no moral obligation to keep a promise not yet given. Critics have considered this to be a novelist's trick for maintaining

the image of the strict and idealistic Dorothea, while not forcing her (as if a real human being) to suffer the pain that her admirable choice would have brought, had she followed this decision. In contrast, Jane Bhandari, unasked, is going through her husband's collection of slides, some with deteriorated colour, trying to restore them, trying to identify the people in them and list them; above all, seeking to understand what her husband would have intended with them.

[14] A famous painting by the English Pre-Raphaelite painter, William Holman Hunt, "The Light of the World" (1851-53), shows Jesus knocking at a dark door (evidently — because it is surrounded with weeds — not used for a very long time) and which has no apparent external means of opening it. It illustrates a passage from the book of Revelations *Behold, I stand at the door, and knock; if any man hear my voice, and open the door, I will come in to him, and will sup with him, and he with me.* The disused and overgrown door is a symbol of the human soul ignorant or impervious to Christ's teaching, and the light from his lantern embodies conscience on the one hand and salvation on the other. (www.janet85.freeserve.co.uk) When a friend commented that he had forgotten to paint a handle on the door, Holman Hunt said, "the handle is on the inside".
This verse is the basis of a poem by devotional English poet George Herbert, "I struck the board and said 'No More'".

[15] See Lewis Carroll (Charles Lutwidge Dodgson (1832-1898)), Through the Looking Glass (1872), Chapter 2.

[16] See also, 'Blind Trust'.

[17] Maria Callas, New York born opera singer, 1923-1977, interview in a bio-pic of her life.

[18] Hong Kong boat people usually put bracelets on little boys, so that, if and when they fall into the water, there is

something to be hooked onto, so that the child can easily be lifted out. Girls are not given such bracelets.

[19] Bocca Tigris.

[20] This example was provided by the writer's husband, Verner Bickley.

[21] "O! reason not the need; our basest beggars
Are in the poorest thing superfluous:
Allow not nature more than nature needs,
Man's life is cheap as beast's. Thou art a lady;
If only to go warm were gorgeous,
Why, nature needs not what thou gorgeous wear'st,
Which scarcely keeps thee warm." (William Shakespeare, *King Lear*, II iv, 274-280.)

[22] A popular 1925 musical, which included the songs, 'Tea for Two' and 'I want to be happy'.

[23] The echo of Edgar Allen Poe's 'The Raven' is a conscious one.

[24] This line was originally written, "going to Heathrow", with the note, "The major international airport in London, United Kingdom."

## Notes to 'Five New Scorchers Blaze a Trail'

[25] Where references are to *poems* in the collections under discussion, the page numbers will be given in parentheses in the main text.

[26] I acknowledge helpful input from colleagues attending the seminar. 

[27] Clare Tyrrell, "Stanza and deliver", *South China Morning Post*, 8 March 2004, C5.

[28] Rosie Milne, "under cover", *Sunday Morning Post*, 14 March 2004.

[29] Nick Gentle, 'Performance poetry steps into the literary limelight', *South China Morning Post*, 9 March 2004, C3.

[30] Matthew Steele, email message to all five "Scorchers", dated 11 March 2004.

[31] 'The Planner', *South China Morning Post*, 24 April 2004, C11.

[32] *South China Morning Post*, 8 March 2004, C1.

[33] Gillian Workman, 'Hong Kong Bibliography' in *Asia/Pacific Literatures in English*, edited by Robert E. McDowell and Judith H. McDowell, Washington, DC, Three Continents Press, 1978, pp. 85-115.

[34] See Gillian Workman, *Ibid*, pp. 88-89.

[35] Dino Mahoney, 'The OutLoud story', *Outloud*, Hong Kong, XtraLoud Press, 2002, pp. 1-8, p. 2.

[36] Mimi Chan accepted 27-years Hong Kong resident, Frederick Stewart (1862-1889) as an "Asian Voice in English" at the conference, "Asian Voices in English", held at Hong Kong University in the 1980s.

[37] Clare Tyrrell, 'Stanza and deliver', *South China Morning Post*, 8 March 2004, C5, c. 5.

[38] Dino Mahoney, *op. cit.*, p. 3.

[39] Present writer's emphasis.

[40] Chinese film actress, the star of *Light the Red Lanterns*.

[41] The last British Governor of Hong Kong.

[42] In the poem of the same name, the "ancient mariner" forces a wedding guest to listen to his story about his senseless killing of an albatross, the punishment that followed, and the forgiveness that he ultimately received. This forgiveness, however, was associated with the unending task of telling his story to others.

[43] Rosanna Wong, President of the Hong Kong Schools Music and Speech Association (HKSM&SA), 'Preface', in, *For the Record and other Poems of Hong Kong*, [pp. 5-6], [p. 5].

[44] *Ibid*, [p. 6].

[45] Louise Ho, 'Foreword', in, Xu Xi and Michael Ingham, eds, *City Voices: Hong Kong Writing in English 1945 to the Present*, Hong Kong, Hong Kong University Press, 2003, pp. xiii-xiv, p. xiii.

[46] Clare Tyrrell, *op. cit.*, cc. 1-2.

[47] Elaine Ho, 'Foreword', in, Timothy Kaiser, *Food Court*, Hong Kong, Chameleon Press, 2004, pp. 11-14, p. 11.

[48] Elaine Ho, *Ibid*, p. 14.

[49] David McKirdly, review of Gillian Bickley, *For the Record*, in, *The Asian Review of Books*.

[50] Shirley Lim, 'Coming ashore for a Wander' [Review of Peter Stambler, *Coming Ashore Far From Home*], *South China Morning Post*, 4 February 2000.

[51] Peter Stambler, *Coming Ashore Far From Home*, Hong Kong, Asia 2000, 2000.

[52] Gillian Workman, *op. cit.*, p. 88.

[53] Louise Ho, 'Foreword', *op. cit.*, p. xiv.

[54] Louise Ho, *Ibid*, p. xiii.

[55] Paradoxically, Shirley Lim's views, expressed in a very able, comprehensive and interesting commentary on poetry and poetic form at the present time, may have taken the direction they have because Stambler's book includes poems, which are versions or constructs based on translations of Han Shan's Tang Dynasty poetry.

# Moving House
## and other Poems from Hong Kong

## From the reviews

From a review of both *Moving House and other Poems from Hong Kong* and *For the Record and other Poems of Hong Kong* by Ian Wotherspoon, in *The Overseas Pensioner* (Official Journal of The Overseas Service Pensioners' Association and The Overseas Service Pensioners' Benevolent Society), UK, No. 91, April 2006, pp. 56-57.

Gillian Bickley's poetry is...fresh, insightful and in rhythm with the sensitivities of a community passing through a period of political and social change. More significantly, it is an important contribution to the evolution of cross-cultural poetry in, and about, Hong Kong...."

**From a review by Solveig Bang**, *Sunday Morning Post*, 4 June 2006

"Gillian Bickley's new book of poetry is not simply a keenly observed collection of Hong Kong scenes, but also a privileged view into the emotional, intellectual and spiritual life of its writer."

"Bickley has lived in Hong Kong for more than 30 years and her public poems, richly peopled with street sweepers and fortune-tellers, hawkers and hairdressers, enable poet and reader to celebrate Hong Kong life."

"pragmatism accompanied by wry wit"

"The studied juxtaposition of the municipal with the personal offers the reader both the familiar...and the private."

"The profound intimacy of the personal poems, reflecting universal truths about the human condition, renders the reader at once intruder and confidant."

"poignant and heart-wrenching observations on ageing and death"

**From a review by "MM",** *Hong Kong Magazine,* 24 November 2006, p. 60.

"Bickley emerges from the poems as a funny, perceptive, caring, and wise person."

**From a review by Paul Bench** in, *Speech & Drama: The Journal of the Society of Teachers of Speech and Drama,* UK, Vol. 56, No. 2, 20006, p. 40.

"images, as if from a poetic camera, of experiences and reflections of existence in Hong Kong"

"the poetic observations of a sensitive writer responding to the reality of being alive"

"insightful probing into the darker issues of our lives . . . to make sense of human experience"

**Review by Tammy Ho** in *Asian Review of Books*, 24 September 2006. (Reproduced by kind permission of Tammy Ho and *Asian Review of Books*.)

~~~Boldly claiming that 'My poems are snapshots of Hong Kong' in the first poem of her latest collection of poetry Moving House And Other Poems From Hong Kong, Gillian Bickley does not exaggerate what many of her 69 delicately-crafted poems achieve. Bickley's poems are faithful word portraits of various aspects of Hong Kong at the turn of the millennium: its landscape, its people, its myths and spirits.

Scattered intermittently among these poems are also the poet's personal responses to life and humanity. In 'Past Present', for example, Bickley comments on the circularity of time: 'We miss the past because we came from there:/ — people and scenes and places, and ways of doing things [...] I embrace the present,/ in embracing you'. And in the final stanza: 'But I/ surely know/ the past is where we also come from;/ and where we're going, too.' Elsewhere, in 'Walking New Paths', Bickley compares old paths that weather with nature and present unexpected views with new cement paths that are characterless, unsurprising, supplying her take on the choices made in this city by virtue of urban development; and the implications of what's lost.

There is also a group of poems in the collection which is about love. In 'Marriage', for example, Bickley offers a different understanding of the ritual, saying that 'marriage is for death': 'death of selfishness, independence, and carelessness;/ death of loneliness, and single nights.' In 'Mutuality', the poet articulates the inseparableness of husband and wife:

*--Twin trees, closely planted,*
*Reach up to the light; reach out to each other.*
*One extends, the other yields.*
*One sheds leaves, the other roots*
*Deeper. The wind blows. They embrace.*
*Each other's anchor in the storm.*

This stanza from 'Mutuality' re-writes and expands on a famous line from a Tang poem about a pair of star-crossed lovers: 'In the sky I wish we fly with same wings; on the earth I wish we are trees with roots linked'.

Love comes in many forms, though all have the potential to surpass time. Bickley writes tenderly about her parents in some of the final poems in *Moving House*. Two poems particularly stand out: 'What I Wanted to Say' is about the final words a daughter wants to say to her dying father, and the impossibility of saying them; the cruelty of death. 'Kindness (A Fragment)' is a recollection of a dream, in which the Mother, now dead, is forever benevolent and caring.

In this collection of poetry about the city, life, love and death, the definitions of prose and poetry blur. Metrical form almost always gives way to the more immediate and natural rhythm of speech.

More than thirty years of residence here result in this collection of poetry written from a deep and devoted insider's perspective. Bickley is more observing than most Hong Kong people who rarely find the time to meditate on the sadness and beauty of this city, and life itself. ~~~

# WRITE TO US!

We are interested to read your comments on
Gillian Bickley's, *Moving House*.
Write to our email address, info@proversepublishing.com,
giving us a few sentences
which you are willing for us to publish,
describing your response to this book.
If your comments are chosen to be included
in our E-Newsletter or website,
we will select another title published by Proverse
and send you a complimentary copy.
When you write to us, please include your name, email
address and correspondence address.
Unless you state otherwise, we will assume that we may cut
or edit your comments for publication.
We will use your initials to attribute your comments.

## ABOUT PROVERSE HONG KONG

Proverse Hong Kong is based in Hong Kong with expanding long-term regional and international connections.

Proverse has published novels, novellas, fictionalized autobiography, non-fiction (including biography, diaries, history, memoirs, sport, travel narratives), single-author poetry collections, children's, teens / young adult and academic books. Other interests include academic works in the humanities, social sciences, cultural studies, linguistics and education. Some Proverse books have accompanying audio texts. Some are translated into Chinese.

Proverse welcomes authors who have a story to tell, wisdom, perceptions or information to convey, a person they want to memorialize, a neglect they want to remedy, a record they want to correct, a strong interest that they want to share, skills they want to teach, and who consciously seek to make a contribution to society in an informative, interesting and well-written way. Proverse works with texts by non-native-speaker writers of English as well as by native English-speaking writers. The name, "Proverse", combines the words "prose" and "verse" and is pronounced accordingly.

## THE PROVERSE PRIZE

The Proverse Prize, an annual international competition for an unpublished book-length work of fiction, non-fiction, or poetry, was established in January 2008. Unusually for a competition of this nature, it is open to all who are at least eighteen on the date they sign the entry form and without restriction of nationality, residence or citizenship.

The objectives of the Proverse Prize are: to encourage excellence and / or excellence and usefulness in publishable written work in the English Language, which can, in varying degrees, "delight and instruct". Entries are invited from anywhere in the world.

Founders: Verner Bickley and Gillian Bickley. To celebrate their lifelong love of words in all their forms as readers, writers, editors, academics, performers, and publishers.
Honorary Legal Advisor: Mr Raymond T. L. Tse.
Honorary Accountant: Mr Neville Chow.
Honorary Judges: Anonymous.
Honorary Advisors: Bahamian poet Marion Bethel; UK linguist & lexicographer David Crystal; Canadian poet and academic, Jonathan Hart; Swedish linguist Björn Jernudd; English translator, Margaret Clarke; Hong Kong University Librarian, Peter Sidorko; Singapore poet Edwin Thumboo; Czech novelist & poet Olga Walló.
Honorary UK agent and distributor: Christine Penney.

*Moving House and Other Poems from Hong Kong 125*

Honorary Administrators: Proverse Hong Kong.
Semi-finalists to date include writers born or resident in Andorra, Australia, Canada, Germany, Hong Kong, New Zealand, Nigeria, Singapore, Taiwan, The Bahamas, the PRC, the United Arab Emirates, the United Kingdom, the USA.

**Proverse Prize Winners whose books have already been published by Proverse Hong Kong:**

Laura Solomon (New Zealand), Rebecca Jane Tomasis (Hong Kong & the United Kingdom); Gillian Jones (United Kingdom); David Diskin (UK and Hong Kong), Peter Gregoire (UK and Hong Kong), Sophronia Liu (Hong Kong and USA); Birgit Linder (Hong Kong, Germany); James McCarthy (Scotland, UK); Celia Claase; Philip Chatting.

**Summary Terms and Conditions**
(for indication only & subject to revision)

The information below is for guidance only. Please refer to the year-specific Proverse Prize Entry Form & Terms & Conditions, which are uploaded, no later than 14 April each year, onto the Proverse Hong Kong website: <www.proversepublishing.com>.

The free Proverse E-Newsletter includes ongoing information about the Proverse Prize.

To be put on the E-Newsletter mailing-list, email: info@proversepublishing.com with your request.

**The Prize**
1) Publication by Proverse Hong Kong, with
2) Cash prize of HKD10,000 (HKD7.80 = approx. US$1.00)

Supplementary publication grants may be made to selected other entrants for publication by Proverse Hong Kong.

Depending on the quality of the work in any year, the prize may be shared by at most two entrants or withheld, as recommended by the judges.

In 2016, the entry fee was: HKD220.00 OR GBP32.00.

Writers are eligible, who are at least eighteen on the date they sign The Proverse Prize entry documents. There is no nationality or residence restriction.

Each submitted work must be an unpublished publishable single-author work of non-fiction, fiction or poetry, the original work of the entrant, and submitted in the English language. School textbooks and plays are ineligible.

Unpublished first translations into English (including those already published in the writer's mother tongue) submitted by the author are welcome. The submitted work will not be judged as a translation but as an original work.

Extent of the Manuscript: within the range of what is usual for the genre of the work submitted. However, it is advisable that novellas be in the range 30,000 to 45,000 words); other fiction (e.g. novels, short-story collections) and non-fiction (e.g. autobiographies, biographies, diaries, letters, memoirs, essay collections, etc.) should be in the range, 75,000 to 100,000 words. Poetry / poetry collections should be in the range, 5,000 to 25,000 words. Other word-counts and mixed-genre submissions are not ruled out.

Writers may choose, if they wish, to obtain the services of an Editor in presenting their work, and should acknowledge this help and the nature and extent of this help in the Entry Form.

The regulations are updated from time to time. Please visit proversepublishing.com for updated entry information.

# KEY DATES FOR THE PROVERSE PRIZE IN ANY YEAR
* (subject to confirmation and/or change)

| | |
|---|---|
| Receipt of Entry Fees / Entry Documents | [No later than] 14 April to 31 May of the year of entry |
| Receipt of entered manuscripts | 1 May to 30 June of the year of entry |
| Announcement of Semi-finalists | * July-September of the year of entry |
| Announcement of Finalists | * October-December of the year of entry |
| Announcement of winner/ max two winners (sharing the cash prize) | December of the year of entry to April of the year that follows the year of entry |
| Cash Award Made | At the same time as publication of the work(s) adjudged the winner / joint-winners of the Proverse Prize |
| Publication of winning work(s) | * In or after November of the year that follows the year of entry |

# THE INTERNATIONAL PROVERSE POETRY PRIZE
## (SINGLE POEMS)

An annual international Proverse Poetry Prize (for single poems) was established in 2016. The international Proverse Poetry Prize is open to all who are at least eighteen years old whatever their residence, nationality or citizenship. Single poems, submitted in English, are invited on (a) any subject or theme, chosen by the writer OR (b) on a subject or theme selected by the organizers from year to year.
Poems may be in any form, style or genre. Each poem should be no more than 30 lines.
Entries should previously be unpublished in any way (except in the case of unpublished translations into English of the entrant's own work already published in another language, providing the entrant holds the copyright, which are eligible).

**In 2016**
**cash prizes were offered as follows:**
**1st prize; USD100.00; 2nd prize: USD45.00;**
**3rd prizes (up to four winners): USD20.00.**

If there are enough good entries in any year, an anthology of prize-winners and selected other entries will be published.
In 2016, judging took place at the same time as the judging for the Proverse Prize for unpublished book-length fiction, non-fiction or poetry.
Judges: anonymous (as for the Proverse Prize for an unpublished book-length work).
Max number of entries per person: No maximum.
No poet may win more than one prize.

**The above information is for guidance only.**
**More information, updated from time to time, is available on**
**the Proverse website: proversepublishing.com**

# KEY DATES FOR THE PROVERSE POETRY PRIZE
## IN 2017 ONWARDS
### (subject to confirmation and/or change)

| | |
|---|---|
| Receipt of entered work and entry fees | 7 May to 14 July of the year of entry |
| Announcement of Winners | October-December of the year of entry up to March-April of the following year |
| Cash Awards Made | At the same time as publication of the winning poems (whether in the Proverse newsletter or website, or in an anthology) |
| Publication of an anthology of winning and other selected entries | Contingent on the quality of entries in any year |

**For more and updated information,
please visit the website: proversepublishing.com**

## POETRY AND POETRY COLLECTIONS
### Published by Proverse Hong Kong

If you have enjoyed *Moving House* by Gillian Bickley, you may also enjoy the following poetry and poetry collections published by Proverse Hong Kong (all titles in English unless otherwise stated):

*Astra and Sebastian*, by L.W. Illsley. 2011.

*Chasing light*, by Patricia Glinton Meicholas. 2013.

*China suite and other poems*, by Gillian Bickley. 2009.

*For the record and other poems of Hong Kong*, by Gillian Bickley. 2003.

*Frida Kahlo's Cry and Other Poems*, by Laura Solomon. 2015.

*Home, away, elsewhere*, by Vaughan Rapatahana. 2011.

*Immortelle and bhandaaraa poems*, by Lelawattee Manoo-Rahming. 2011.

*In vitro*, by Laura Solomon. 2nd ed. 2014.

*Irreverent Poems for Pretentious People*, by Henrik Hoeg. 2016.

*Moving house and other poems from Hong Kong*, by Gillian Bickley. 2005.

*Of Leaves & Ashes*, by Patty Ho. *2016.*

*Of symbols misused*, by Mary-Jane Newton. 2011.

*Moving House and Other Poems from Hong Kong    131*

*Painting the borrowed house: poems*, by Kate Rogers. 2008.

*Perceptions*, by Gillian Bickley. 2012.

*Rain on the pacific coast*, by Elbert Siu Ping Lee. 2013.

*refrain*, by Jason S. Polley. 2010.

*Shadow play*, by James Norcliffe. 2012.

*Shadows in Deferment*, by Birgit Bunzel Linder, 2013.

*Shifting Sands*, by Deepa Vanjani. 2016.

*Sightings: a collection of poetry, with an essay, 'communicating poems'*, by Gillian Bickley. 2007.

*Smoked pearl: poems of Hong Kong and beyond*, by Akin Jeje (Akinsola Olufemi Jeje). 2010.

*The Layers Between* (Essays and Poems), by Celia Claase. 2015.

*Unlocking*, by Mary-Jane Newton. March 2014.

*Wonder, lust & itchy feet*, by Sally Dellow. 2011.

## POETRY – CHINESE LANGUAGE

*For the record and other poems of Hong Kong*, by Gillian Bickley. Translated by Simon Chow. 2010.

*Moving house and other poems from Hong Kong, translated into Chinese, with additional material*, by Gillian Bickley. Edited by Tony Ming-Tak Yip. Translated by Tony Yip & others. 2008.

## FIND OUT MORE ABOUT OUR AUTHORS BOOKS AND EVENTS, THE PROVERSE PRIZE, AND THE PROVERSE POETRY PRIZE

**Visit our website**
http://www.proversepublishing.com
**Visit our distributor's website**
<www.chineseupress.com>

**Follow us on Twitter**
Follow news and conversation:
<twitter.com/Proversebooks>
*OR*
Copy and paste the following to your browser window and follow the instructions:
https://twitter.com/#!/ProverseBooks

**"Like" us on www.facebook.com/ProversePress**

**Request our E-Newsletter**
Send your request to info@proversepublishing.com.

## Availability

Most titles are available in Hong Kong and world-wide
from our Hong Kong based Distributor,
The Chinese University Press of Hong Kong,
The Chinese University of Hong Kong, Shatin, NT,
Hong Kong SAR, China. Web: chineseupress.com

All titles are available from Proverse Hong Kong
and the Proverse Hong Kong UK-based Distributor.

We have stock-holding retailers in Hong Kong,
Singapore (Select Books),
Canada (Elizabeth Campbell Books),
Principality of Andorra (Llibreria La Puça, La Llibreria).
Orders can be made from bookshops
in the UK and elsewhere.


## Ebooks

Most of our titles are available also as Ebooks.

www.ingramcontent.com/pod-product-compliance
Lightning Source LLC
Chambersburg PA
CBHW071351090426
42738CB00012B/3081